INTELLIGENCE AND DEMOCRATIC ACTION

Lectures delivered at the
Thomas Jefferson Center
for Studies in Political Economy
University of Virginia

INTELLIGENCE AND
DEMOCRATIC ACTION

by Frank H. Knight

HARVARD UNIVERSITY PRESS
Cambridge, Massachusetts · 1960

FOREWORD

The lectures published in this volume were delivered at the Thomas Jefferson Center for Studies in Political Economy at the University of Virginia during the first half of 1958. During this period Professor Knight served at the Center as the Inaugural Distinguished Visiting Scholar. The lectures are being published because we believe that the ideas presented here deserve a much wider audience than a university lecture series normally affords.

It should be emphasized that these are published lectures. They were transcribed from tapes recorded during the actual presentation, edited by the staff of the Center, and somewhat hastily revised by Professor Knight. This volume is not "the book" that Professor Knight would have written, and that we hope he will write, as a definitive treatment of this critical topic of the age. It is instead, as he would say, an extended preface. But such an informal statement of views has definite advantages of its own, serving to complement the more formal treatise that we hope will be forthcoming.

We need not introduce Professor Knight to the large group of scholars who have benefited from the many contributions he has made during his long and distinguished scholarly career. To those others who may be encountering

Frank Knight here for the first time, this little book serves as ample introduction. Any brief words on our part would be presumptuous as well as unnecessary.

James M. Buchanan

G. Warren Nutter

Charlottesville, Virginia
August 27, 1959

CONTENTS

INTELLIGENCE AND
DEMOCRATIC ACTION

Chapter I ~ THE QUEST
FOR RATIONAL NORMS

The assignment in this series of lectures calls for saying something worth saying about intelligent or wise decisions on economic policies in a democratic state. That requires steering between two extremes; to use the Homeric cliché, between the Scylla of the excessively trite and trivial and the Charybdis of analysis too intricate or technical to be followed by anyone not a narrow specialist. (And the reader may again be reminded that they were originally intended for oral presentation.) That dilemma will be "barking at our heels" all the way through, for it lies at the heart of the task. The most important obligation of the teacher of economics who seriously tries to be useful in the way indicated by the title of this series is to get the public, the electorate, to pay attention to and apply self-evident truths or virtual truisms. The situation suggests as a primary need some Gertrude Stein to reiterate that an exchange is an exchange is an exchange. A democracy is dedicated to freedom, and an exchange is free by definition; if a transaction is not free for both parties, it is not an exchange. And that means that it is of advantage to both, if they are competent to manage their own affairs, an assumption that goes with that of democracy. In practice, it means not ideally competent but more so than the political functionaries who will otherwise manage for them. In this connection I often think of a saying of a once popular American humorist, known by the pen-name of Josh Billings, to the effect that it isn't ignorance that does the most damage, but knowin' so derned much that ain't so. Worse still, it is not error either, for the people in question really know quite well the falsity and absurdity of what they say, or of the premises on which it obviously rests.

In short, the major, logically preliminary, task is to overcome *prejudice*; and a good deal must be said as we proceed about that concept or category and its sub-species. In the nature of the case it is hard to define at all objectively. The usual and natural reference is to a view expressed by someone else, with which "I"—the particular speaker or writer—disagree. However, a direct imputation of prejudice to an opponent in argument is immediately destructive of the spirit of discussion, and to achieve and maintain that intellectual attitude is the first essential. Lord Bryce defined democracy as "government by discussion," and discussion itself must be a main topic for discussion in dealing with our general subject. Now, discussion also is inherently free— in fact it may be viewed as a form of exchange, and rather the most fundamental form. The two activities are closely associated in economic relations, and together make up the ideal-type which defines free association. In so far, that is, as this is intelligent; this term also needs much defining, specifically in relation to freedom, the concept that is at the focus of controversy.

Thus the fact that exchange is always free merely raises the major problems. It by no means implies that freedom of exchange is a general answer to questions of policy. We cannot take as axiomatic either that it is itself always a good thing—that depends on many conditions in real life—or that much coercive action is not required to maintain the nearest possible approximation to the theoretical pattern, as in general freedom can be effective only if restricted by law. It is not even true without important exceptions that the individual is competent to manage his own affairs, or more competent than a governmental agency, as these are and may be expected to be. One is not always the best judge of one's own well-being, and still less can this be separated from the well-being of others or, more especially of "society" and of civilization in the large and in the long view.

Enough has been said to indicate that we confront a mixture of pseudo-problems with real ones, of the greatest complexity and subtlety. Accordingly, the lectures must find virtue in the Aristotelian fashion, by steering between opposite evils. Of the two, being too technical, or too "philosophical," is perhaps more easily avoided than being commonplace. Either is a deadly sin from the standpoint of effective communication; but neither can be entirely avoided, since the same statement that is trivial to one mind may be obscure or meaningless to another—or repugnant as a reminder of truth that is opposed by some prejudice. This I think is especially true in economics, especially as regards avoiding what is or ought to be triviality. Through four decades of struggle to understand and expound the essentials of the subject, I have been increasingly impressed by the fact that the most important substance should not need to be taught. We spend our time and wear away our lives triturating the obvious; we hardly get to the point where real problems begin; we are in the position that has been described as "reaching up to touch bottom." In an effort to separate real from bogus problems, and say something about the real ones, much of what must be said will be little more than preaching, exhorting people to use good sense, look objectively at facts, see what the problems are and approach them intelligently, as problems. Much of it must be negative rather than constructive—what not to do, especially much that has been and is done, and exposing the nonsensical arguments used to defend the indefensible. In fact, I see as the main task of general education to "unteach," to overcome prejudice and the inclination to snap judgments and develop the will to be intelligent, i.e., objective and critical.

This situation, I repeat, is particularly striking in the field of economics. One reason is that the attitude of using means "rationally"—to achieve ends under a maximizing principle —is a new thing in history. And a critical or questioning attitude toward ends is newer still, while if we speak of social ends, it is only now struggling to be born. These innovations have followed in succession since it became permissible to question established dogma accepted as describing and explaining phenomena in the field of physical nature, i.e., after the end of the Middle Ages. They are principal features in the "Liberal Revolution," discussed in the second lecture. In economics, inquiry and discussion are opposed by an age-old inherited tradition of antagonism to almost every feature of a free economic order—to trade, property, profit and all gain-seeking, lending at interest, even to giving employment to labor on terms made possible by what it will produce, under direction which makes it boundlessly more productive than ever before, or than it could be otherwise. This antagonism is even deeply embedded in our religion. Woe is pronounced on the rich and those who would be rich, who stand no chance of entering the Kingdom of Heaven; it is wrong to lend, expecting any return, and even to be concerned about the morrow, specifically as regards food and clothing; money is the root of all evil, and the one righteous use of wealth is giving it to the poor. This is a ticklish subject to discuss, but is too relevant and important to be ignored. Apart from religion, costs and money-matters belong to those facts-of-life which it is hardly respectable to talk about openly. This prejudice, a survival from past ages, calls for a historical view of liberal culture, which will be sketched in the following lecture and noticed again in the final one of the series.

*   *   *

It seems appropriate, and perhaps not too boring, to mention two perennial examples of stupidity in economic ideas and policy—stupidity reflecting prejudice rather than intellectual error or ignorance. One is protectionism in foreign trade; the other is inflation, the idea and policy of creating wealth or prosperity by making money abundant and cheap, that is, making it available at an artificially low interest-rate. Both fallacies have been stock bad-examples to economists, by virtually unanimous agreement, since the science was founded, some two centuries ago. It happens that in politics in this country, the first fallacy has been promoted by one of our main parties, and the second one by the other, so that bracketing the two may sidestep the accusation that I myself am prejudiced in that respect. The decisive matter for the analyst is the kind of arguments used in such cases, since political arguing is the method by which issues are decided in a democratic society. The arguments employed are presumably expected to be effective, and issues of action are of course decided by those that actually prevail—their relation to "truth" being the main problem here. Not only is what passes for argument largely an appeal to prejudice but it also consists in great part in imputing prejudice to opponents. Criticisms range from accusations of outright intent to deceive for promoting some selfish interest, all the way to general character denunciation. Such accusing and moralizing must in due course be considered as a trait of human nature and a leading source of corruption of objective thinking.

As regards protectionism, I shall inject a personal note. My own inherited bias was in favor of this fallacy, since as a toddler, I toddled under a Republican table, on a farm in the Middle West. (Incidentally, a majority of this "class" voted for protectionism, directly against their own economic interest.) I recall how hard it was for me to get free from this prejudice, which I actually did as a student of economics at the university level. My political memory now goes rather far back, to the McKinley-Bryan campaign of 1896, where protectionism and cheap money were the leading issues. I recall a Republican campaign speech that exploited the hoary piece of nonsense that if Americans buy from foreigners, a foreign country gets the money and America the goods, but if they buy from Americans, America has the goods and the money both. Such reasoning raises the question whether there is any use in pointing out facts, whether one merely insults one's own intelligence by casting pearls before, let us say, beings oblivious to their value. Such doubts are hardly lessened by noting that partisans on the other side seem to see the truth here, but fall for other fallacies equally egregious, notably the other of the pair mentioned, cheap money. The campaign referred to saved the country from prosperity through inflation and from the impoverishment of American labor through allowing consumers to buy from the most efficient producers. One may recall Bastiat's mock petition of the candle-makers for a prohibition of windows, to exclude the ruinous competition of cheap foreign light from the sun—and the fact that this *reductio ad absurdum* produced no visible effect.

The case of inflation is as simple, in principle. Money serves only to get valuable things away from other people, and obviously, if everyone were given more money in equal proportions, no one would be any better off. All prices would merely be that much higher and the only effects would be a partial nullification of contracts and some transitional disorganization of the market system. Further analysis is not in point here. The task of the serious student interested in general economic well-being is to understand the thinking illustrated, particularly that it rests more on "honest" prejudice than on a deliberate effort to promote selfish interests, though both are involved. At bottom, the same two or three prejudices underlie both our cases. One is the "money illusion," confusing money with real wealth. More general is the failure, or refusal, to recognize that free exchange is axiomatically advantageous to both parties, if they have elementary competence to manage their own affairs (and barring "force and fraud"). Coupled with this is the assumption that "the government" is a sort of benevolent god with the role of compelling people to act in accord with their real interest, which they as individuals misunderstand or perversely misconceive. All this, however, by no means proves that a policy of extreme governmental passivity (*laisser faire*) is the right or best solution for the general problems of economic relations. As we shall see, this is very far from being the case. Meanwhile, it may be noted that the trend in public economic thinking and action is far from encouraging. In our generation and in most of the world, both protection and inflation have gone from bad to worse—aggravated by the mania of economic nationalism, another virulent prejudice. And in addition, these venerable follies have been rather surpassed by such new and obvious stupidities as a farm program which overtly subsidizes the production of surpluses—and then causes more needless waste in getting rid of them instead of, say, simply and immediately burning them up. Moreover, this is done to aid people with no claim to help from others, and largely at the expense of the consumers of necessaries more in a position to make such a claim than to meet it. Again, one must doubt the utility of argument, of explaining to people who can read and write and do elementary arithmetic, that arbitrarily fixing a price above that which will equalize the amount demanded with the forthcoming supply must have the effect we see—and the opposite policy the opposite one of creating a shortage and requiring some mode of arbitrary rationing. Rather worse still is the popular idea that the wages of labor (of workers as a class) can be artificially raised above the value of the individual's contribution to the total product, measured by the free choices of consumers except by an arbitrary exaction from somebody else, but this again does not mean that no individual's or family's scale of living should ever be raised by a subsidy, to be assessed equitably and so managed as to minimize the distortion of market relations. The prejudice underlying this fallacy is somewhat different from those previously noted. It is rooted in the absurd belief that only labor is productive, and any share going to property owners, or to such as happen to make profit over some interval, is filched from the just earnings of labor and represents extortion.

The task of an introduction to our general theme is especially hard. A preliminary survey presents in an aggravated form the difficulties of the series, which itself can only be a somewhat more detailed survey of a vast and vaguely definable field. Without attempting to deal very specifically with particular and positive issues, the objective will be to indicate the underlying problems which create the difficulties in the way of intelligent policy determination—in a society dedicated to maximum individual freedom and, in social action, to the methods of democratic politics. Much of what is said here must be repeated later, in more detail. Repetition is not always bad; I often recall an observation of Herbert Spencer, that only by varied iteration can alien truths be impressed upon reluctant minds. The most important truth in question is the alien quality of truth in this field, and the reluctance of the typical mind to see and face obvious truths, when they run counter to a prejudice. The role of conscious self-seeking, distinct from formally sincere belief, is not much considered here, as I believe it to be quite secondary in importance. The difficulty is that of separating the two, because of a vast capacity in human nature on the one hand to believe in accord with a selfish interest, and on the other to make any opinion, once formed in any way, into an interest on its own account. Man is an opinionated animal, and contentious, as well as romantic (uncritical) in forming opinions. This is true in all fields of knowledge, but especially in those dealing with people and institutions, and most notably with respect to value judgments. In consequence, the need for intelligence in a democratic society confronts a dis-harmony within human nature.

Another difficulty is that democracy presents such a complex of problems and so intertwined that far too much needs to be said about them if one says anything true and relevant, and much of it needs to be said "first," as preliminary to the rest. Hence there cannot be any very logical order in the presentation and, again, much repetition is needful, to bring particular statements into relation with different contexts.

In view of all that has been said so far, one thing needing to be said before going farther is to issue a warning, not to expect too much. In general, the particular romantic prejudice of unreasonable expectations causes much needless discontent, and menace to order. Carlyle remarked that if men were convinced that they deserved to be hanged, they would consider it a luxury to be shot. Conceit, exaggeration of one's merits, generates an expectation of being treated accordingly by one's fellows, society, and the world, which is sure to be largely disappointed. The world shows no evidence of a concern for either justice or mercy, and in large-scale society this human attitude toward the individual spreads slowly and fitfully outward from the family, and is not yet reliable even there. Men need above all to learn to be reasonably satisfied with the possible, which means possible progress, beginning with progressively knowing what it means and how to achieve it, and not expecting any solution for social problems. The prior objective is to avoid false solutions, or remedies worse than the diseases they are intended to cure or alleviate. That achievement is so far in the future that one is inclined to settle for negative action, less that is indefensibly stupid, postponing attack on positive and properly controversial issues until the bogus ones are disposed of. People must be educated out of unreasonable expectations from the economic order, and especially from the political order as an agency for remedying its defects, real or supposed.

It is a romantic delusion that we would want our problems solved: what would we do then? Of course there is no danger of that; the danger is rebelliousness from irrational expectations and discontent. Again, the romanticism in question is deeply embedded in our religious tradition. The conventional picture of the Heavenly Kingdom is a domain without progress or change, with no problems, personal or social. Its social order has never been conceived as a democracy, to say nothing of free enterprise—nor as very inclusive; "many are called, but few are chosen."

Under the head of false and illusory solutions, two in particular need to be stressed. One, to which human nature is conspicuously inclined, is moralizing, finding the cause of our ills in "sin"—chiefly other people's—with the remedy in punishing the bad-men, or "liquidating" them, or burning them alive as heretics, to use historical-Christian terms in place of Marxian. (Marxism has been well called a Christian heresy by a leading Christian theologian.) Exceptionally it has been one's own sin, leading to hatred of oneself as well as the world, sometimes to self-destruction. The relation between sin and error has played a fundamental role in our history, and will call for notice later. Recently the moralistic view has been widely replaced by the second fallacy referred to, which is equally indefensible. That is "scientificism," the notion that social problems can be solved by applying the methods by which man has achieved increasing mastery over nature. But obviously, the basic problems are value problems, to which natural science has little relevance. To begin with, scientific knowledge confers power, but has little to say about the ends for which power is to be used, even by an individual. It shows *how* to do things, how to achieve a concretely defined objective, not what objectives to pursue. Further and more important, in a society dedicated to freedom, power of men over other men is inherently evil, even if exercised with "good intentions," which is not very likely to be the case. Such power is to be minimized, as well as restricted in use, though it is not wholly avoidable and is often a necessary expedient, to avoid evils worse than limiting personal liberty. The relation between freedom and power is obviously a main problem for analysis of the way democratic society operates or how its operation may be improved will be considered especially in my concluding lecture. Again, I warn that I shall offer no definite solutions, but strive only to clarify issues. Concrete measures must be left to that insidious and wily animal, the statesman or politician—to use the language of Adam Smith, who was no advocate of democracy as we understand it. In a society such as ours, the statesman or politician is finally the common man, the whole body of the citizens, meaning all normal adults.

No general solution is to be expected, or even desired. As one of my revered teachers of economics, "Tommy" Adams remarked, no problem is to be dismissed as impossible if it must be solved and for which some solutions are better than others—or at least some are worse. For obvious reasons, I can only stress general principles, one of which is to avoid excessive or misplaced reliance on principles. They may be fairly definitive as to what not to do, but never tell concretely what to do; as to that, there are always opposing principles or reasons for and against any course of action, which must be critically compared. The cynical but wise

Talleyrand has said that the only good principle is to have no principles (*le seul bon principe est de n' en avoir aucun*); what he should have said is that it is good to have many principles, and to take account of all that are relevant, but use judgment as to when and how far and in what way to follow each. Their chief positive use is to indicate lines of factual investigation and define possible alternatives to be appraised. Negatively, as to economic policy, one surely may categorically condemn vote-buying with money extracted from tax-payers—the real nature of some of the measures previously cited for illustration, rather than economic policies, properly speaking.

The democratic action of chief concern here is action *upon* "business," and the way in which it sets problems *for* "politics." These terms, as commonly uttered in a somewhat contemptuous tone (hence the quotation-marks) suggest another fundamental observation. It is clearly stupid for believers in a free society to condemn politicians, in power or seeking office, for using the arguments that will actually win votes, hence are a condition for any success in politics, or accomplishing anything by democratic methods. And the same statement applies (*mutatis mutandis*) to the business man, and also to the labor-leader in any lawful activity. If manifestly wrong things are done or successfully advocated by democratically chosen leaders, the remedy is to educate the public to make or agree upon more intelligent choices of measures and the agents for their administration—or, in the case of business, choice among the goods and services offered for sale. The first step is to make people in general more *critical,* less *romantic,* in their judgments of debating arguments used in political campaigns, and of advertising and sales-talk. The distinctive virtue for men in free society, the essence of the whole liberal view of life, is truth-seeking. The primary axiom for conduct in general is that it is unwise to act unless action can be based on *intelligent* belief and choice among critically appraised alternative possibilities, and the second is the injunction to act when this condition is fulfilled. For, human nature and the given conditions of human life make the chances overwhelming that action directed by impulse or snap judgment, or in response to any irrational emotional appeal, will have consequences that are, on balance, more bad than good.

Since all action involves some change in previous practice, what has been said implies a "conservative" attitude; conservatism, however, is not antithetical to liberalism, but another aspect of it. Conservatism does not mean opposition to all change, but change when and only when there are valid grounds for believing that a particular change will be for the better, that is, will promote "progress." The liberal faith is that progress, improvement, will be achieved through freedom—in contrast on the one hand with change directed by an authority with arbitrary power, and on the other with change made at random or in response to any thoughtless impulse or irrational motive. Liberals hold that men are not to be trusted, beyond necessity, with arbitrary power. As Lord Acton said, power corrupts—corrupts the initially good—and absolute power corrupts absolutely. But weakness in the face of power corrupts equally and apart from consequences, both the power-seeking attitude and that of servility are inherently to be condemned.

With respect to political action in the economic sphere, the main task of society, at the present juncture, is *education,* but of the will more than the intellect; it is to develop a more critical attitude. It is primarily to teach the obvious, what normally competent adults really know already, or would know if they tried to be objective and to develop the will to act with due regard to facts and principles that are not in dispute. But behind and underlying concrete issues of economic policy lie deeper problems, of the nature of intelligent group action, which are my chief concern in these lectures. But they can be considered only rather superficially. Even in a university group, with considerable education in the relevant special fields, within the limits of time more philosophical problems can only be indicated. Adequate discussion would require much defining of terms and drawing distinctions between concepts; and this procedure soon becomes tedious even to one who attempts it, and boring to an audience, particularly in oral presentation. Yet some of it is of the essence of seeking rational norms, hence something must be said about the meaning of a few key terms.

Especially in point is "freedom," the term and the concept. Its synonym, "liberty" is the root of "liberal" and "liberalism," which latter, with the correlative "conservatism" have just been noticed. These two are especially important because of the general inversion of meaning which liberalism has recently undergone in current usage, particularly in this country. Within easy memory of those now in middle life, it stood for freedom, the original and proper meaning; but now it usually has the opposite reference, to governmental paternalism.

A corresponding ambiguity affects freedom itself, and the misleading use must at least be pointed out. Freedom having become a word to conjure with, hence useful for political propaganda, it tends to be extended to cover other values, regardless of the most obvious conflicts of these with freedom, and used to promote social action said to lead to any allegedly good result. Thus a wide variety of programs are supported by defining the objective into freedom itself. In fact, freedom is now commonly so defined by partisans on the two sides of nearly any issue as to beg the question in favor of the desired conclusion. The major fallacy— doubtless responsible for the inversion referred to in the meaning of liberalism—is to hold that one is not free, unless he has the *power* to do anything he would like to do, or to get anything he wants, and has a right to have, or to be free from, any alleged wrong. A good end would then justify use of any effective and necessary means, ignoring bad results also likely to follow from political compulsion. The famous four freedoms proposed by Roosevelt and Churchill as objectives in the recent war, afford an egregious example. More detailed analysis must be postponed (to Lecture V); but it may be pointed out here that freedom and power are different dimensions of voluntary action, and that the view in question virtually makes it the obligation of the state to satisfy everybody—at the expense of everybody else. Governmental action involves compulsion—else it would not be needed—and must be discussed chiefly in relation to concrete issues, which usually are a matter of how much and of how, in detail; they cannot be decided by any simple general formula.

At this point it is appropriate to note briefly some major conflicts of literal individual freedom with other social values or ideas. First of all, "the" *supreme* value is *order*. This is of the essence of any society, prior to freedom and all others. The question is "what" order, and how much—since any rigid order excludes all freedom, and all intelligent action, as such. Another value, currently much in controversy, is *security;* this is logically implied by order, and accordingly clashes with freedom. In fact, freedom for one member of society means disorder and insecurity for others with whom he has dealings. Freedom, being freedom to make changes, implies *progress,* but progress also conflicts with order, and hence with literal freedom. Further, a social order must provide for *economic efficiency,* as one of its main functions, and the relation between efficiency and freedom (and security) creates hard problems. Lastly, in this list, a human social order faces inescapably the problem of *justice,* specifically here, economic or distributive justice. It is an ideal very hard even to define and, human nature being as it is, inevitably conflicts with freedom and its associated values. Finally, beyond these specific value conflicts, we must note inherent limitations of freedom itself. Apart from more metaphysical considerations, it has no meaning for infants, or for adults in so far as they are helpless, which is a matter of degree. Freedom is empty without power to act—though as just shown the two must not be identified—and it also presupposes desires or interests known to the choosing subject. Knowledge of ends is one factor in economic rationality; a subtler question is the relation of freedom to the other factor, knowledge of means and techniques for their use. Children and other dependents, who control no means, must be supported decently, for which voluntary charity will not suffice, thus necessitating compulsion on near relatives and taxation of others supposedly in a position to bear it.

To have freedom, men must in general use it intelligently, or at least not too irrationally. "Intelligent" is preferable to "rational," because ability to reason logically, as in elementary mathematics, is much less rare than sound critical judgment, particularly judgment in choosing ends. And besides, both logical thinking and economic—that is, instrumental—rationality are easily overdone; the American economist, John M. Clark, has observed that an irrational passion for dispassionate rationality would take all the joy out of life.

Men need to be aware of their natural romanticism and to be skeptical of remedies, and first of all diagnoses. This applies even to physical ailments, but much more to social. The role of mind in illness, and the vogue of psychotherapy are much in point, but that subject can only be mentioned here. In several respects, the analogy between physical and social "medicine" is instructive. Among many recorded definitions of "man" one that contains both wit and truth comes from Sir William Osler: he is the animal that takes medicine. But as regards rationality, this field is notoriously infected with snap judgments, magic and superstition, and weird forms of wish-thinking. An eminent student of medicine and its history was recently asked at what date he would guess that doctors began to cure more patients than they killed; after some reflection he answered sadly that perhaps it would be in the future by a generation or so. Of course human longevity and health have been greatly improved in recent times, chiefly in a few Western countries. Without going into the how and why of that, I venture the opinion, or guess, that even with the geographical restriction (certainly for the world as a whole) but including all medical treatment by whomever prescribed, it is still true that "doctoring" does more harm than good.

A similar question may be asked with respect to other conduct, and in my opinion the answer, for many fields, would stress human irrationality more than intelligence.

With respect to physical and biological science, where knowledge is most objective, and with respect to technology based on such knowledge, I shall say more in my next lecture, on historical background. The main fact to be stressed is that the effort to be critically objective is of recent origin, and has made headway against the most strenuous opposition, particularly from the custodians of "truth" as sacred and hence unchanging. One need only mention the name of Galileo, and particularly of Darwin—a reminder that in the public mind this negative advance is still by no means fully achieved. In the field of knowledge requisite for intelligent social action, the new attitude has spread slowly indeed. Some conscious social (political) action has become so obviously necessary that no realistic statement is possible comparing actual conditions with what they would be in its complete absence. But as to economic policy, the illustrations given earlier show that the action taken by our own democracy, and the beliefs of the great majority on which the action rests, are often absurd. Nor are they to be explained by economic self-interest, since the measures depend on votes of electors whose interests are directly opposed to them, as well as of those benefited. The most important matter, I repeat, is the character of the arguments that are used and seem to be effective. In large part these are so obviously fallacious or irrelevant, so question-begging, that it seems quite futile to advance real arguments in opposition.

A general human proclivity for romanticism—including all interests in conflict with the quest of truth—hardly needs demonstration. Within wide limits, human nature clearly finds many forms of fiction more interesting than truth. An esthetically competent painting or drawing, even a caricature, is esteemed above a photograph, as poetry and lyrical prose—well characterized as painting with words—have more appeal than sober statement of fact. Verbal communication on the whole is intentionally more figurative than literally accurate; objective precision is more or less, and often decisively, subordinated to "art," including "craft," that is, use as a means of producing an effect, good or bad. When the effect intended is unmistakably mere entertainment or amusement, this is harmless and may be all to the good. The question then is one of taste, but it raises the serious issue of the role of good and bad taste, in contrast with that "mere" taste, about which there is properly no argument—a matter too subtle for discussion here. The "effect" in question with respect to social action is the replacement of disagreement by agreement—agreement on a "sound" conclusion as far as possible, but it is agreement that is strictly necessary. And the question for democracy is, how far agreement on right or truth, or finally the agreement requisite for peace and order, is to be expected from free discussion if the type of argument that now so widely prevails in business and politics is not vastly improved.

Beyond this first objective in these lectures—warning against romanticism—the second, fully as important, is to stress the *limitations* of the knowledge existent in our society, or likely to be attained, that would be needful for intelligent social action. I speak of necessary knowledge, repeating the reminder that I do not go into the problem of enforcing laws accepted as right, or the best to be had, and as needing enforcement. Later lectures, especially the second and the last, will offer some reflections on the problem of knowledge, that is, "warranted" belief or good judgment—for knowledge can never be absolute. At this point, I merely note that the knowledge needful for intelligent action may be subdivided under three or four heads. In the first place—though the order of listing is somewhat arbitrary—an intelligently acting subject, individual or group in any situation where means are used to achieve ends must know, "predict," what will or would happen in the absence of any action on its part, that is, the "natural" course of events. Secondly, he must know what action is possible, the things he "can do," in the circumstances, with the "given" available means and capacities at his command. Thirdly, he must know what consequences are to be expected from acting in each of the possible ways—another prediction, akin to the first listed. Finally, he must know, correctly appraise, the comparative desirability of all these several consequences, including the natural course of events. That is, as regards this last, he must have a *scale of values* for ranking the various possibilities.

It is to be noted as almost universally the case that right choice among values is not one of all-or-none of each, but the *best combination*. The question is how far to carry the pursuit of any value, initially more important, before some other will begin to exceed it in importance, and the problem becomes one of *proportioning* conflicting values. There are few, if any, absolute imperatives, positive or negative. The desideratum is to maximize value on the whole, which axiomatically is done by carrying different components to the point of equal importance of "marginal" increments which are open alternatives under all the given conditions. That is, the principle familiar in economics is generally applicable, even in fields popularly excluded from that domain—specifically morals and esthetics (the good and the beautiful); and to be finally included are science and philosophy, where "truth" is pursued for its own sake, as an end. (I have in mind the traditional tripartite classification, here followed without the criticism to which it might be subjected.) All values are in principle economic, in so far as their pursuit involves use of means in any form, which may serve a plurality of ends and hence require apportionment among these. All problems are finally value problems, and practically all values are subject to "diminishing utility" (or importance).

In this connection, a vital distinction must be drawn, though it cannot be done with much precision. The term "value" is ambiguous in ordinary usage, particularly as to its relation to "fact." For economics, strictly defined as individualistic, value means private subjective wants, of which the individual is the final judge, and which he is supposed to know intuitively, and quantitatively. But social action requires agreement on important values, to be reached through free discussion; hence they must be treated as *objective,* to be intellectually appraised. The occasion for social action is some conflict of individual interests, and mere assertion by the respective parties of conflicting interests can only intensify the conflict, not tend to agreement, which usually involves compromise. For discussion, private interests must be appraised in terms of their "importance," that is, of what is *desirable* or "ought" to be desired and done, a category in strong contrast with what is merely desired. This objectivity holds for all belief or judgment, as "valid," for all questions which a society regards as needing to be answered on a social scale, by agreement. Human knowledge is social knowledge. Moral questions, what action is not merely instrumentally expedient but also right, would hardly arise for an isolated individual, a Crusoe. Questions of good taste might do so, and those of truth certainly would, but with a special limited pragmatic meaning. For him, truth would be purely instrumental to his given desires, in accord with Hume's dictum that reason is the slave of the passions. But this is clearly not true in civilized society, unless desires for truth and right for their own sake (as well as beauty and various forms of propriety) are included among the passions, and intelligence must also comparatively appraise passions in conflict.

* * *

As it is rather needless to point out, social action is political action, and to be genuinely social it must be democratic; that is, decisions must finally be reached through discussion, with free and equal participation of all members of the society, meaning all normal adults. It is also obvious that all social issues are at bottom questions of what is "good," for society; that is, they are moral or, rather, ethical. These terms are close synonyms in current usage, but a vital distinction needs to be drawn, and somehow recognized in our terminology. The word "moral" properly refers to the *mores,* or that part of socially established customs which is covered by law, law that is felt as compulsive and is enforced by sanctions of some kind. These are to be contrasted first, of course, with scientific laws, and especially with such laws as those of the language spoken, which people obey half-consciously, and also with the laws of manners to which they strive to conform because of informal sanctions of neighborly approval and disapproval. Only a vague distinction is possible between these last two species and moral laws, which are more consciously recognized and discussed and more strenuously enforced, but still informally, not by prescribed penalties. Law in the narrower, jural sense is further distinguished as that part of moral law which is formally enforced, as suggested, by some provision for specific punishment for infractions.

Throughout most of the history of human social life, both the content of the jural laws and authority for their enforcement have been traditional. They have "just growed," like Topsy, without deliberate action. They changed, but slowly and unobserved, as language and manners change through time, by "drift," in the jargon of linguists. As there was no thought of changing them, the jural laws also presented no social problem. Gradually, however, in the course of ages, their substance and procedure came to be criticized and so to present probems—first undoubtedly, within a small ruling class, as to the nature and origin of which we need not speculate. The notion of right (as the English word is used) became differentiated from that of jural legality, and came to be more or less explicitly considered by the authorities in applying the law to cases. (More will be said about the history in the next lecture, but it must remain largely a matter of speculation.) Prior to this development the right was defined once and for all by the jural law which was, in theory, to be enforced without change. The authorities no doubt discriminated more or less consciously as to what laws they would enforce, and how, and made law to some extent. But the pretense that it was found and merely interpreted and applied, has persisted—most remarkably in the English common law—well down into recent times, long after the establishment of a separate legislative organ, the Parliament. (The sovereign "in" Parliament; the former had long had considerable tacitly recognized legislative power.)

In modern democratic societies, laws are largely and

freely made, meaning that changes are deliberately introduced. This fact gives rise to the historically new problem
of the social good (better and worse) to be embodied in the
laws, themselves subject to improvement. This problem of
The Good as dynamic, to be intelligently redefined, of
"progressive" morals, needs a term to distinguish the concept
from morals as the *mores,* viewed as given, unchangeable,
static, and as underlying and justifying the law, similarly
conceived. For this concept and problem-field, clearly requiring a distinctive verbal designation, "ethics" seems to
be the best available term, even though its use for the
purpose involves considerable redefinition, compared with
current usage.

The historical differentiation of forms of law suggests
some further observations. Both the substantive law and the
position, powers, and rights of the enforcing authorities
were, in pre-liberal ages, sanctioned (literally, made sacred)
by the general belief that what was established was supernaturally ordained; nonconformity and disobedience would
be punished by supernatural spiritual powers. Punishment
would also be visited on any society tolerating infraction,
not merely on the guilty individuals. Correspondingly, quite
generally if not always and from the beginning, legal
authority itself has been divided, between a priesthood—
primitive, "church"—and secular "political" leaders, a form
of "state." The latter probably arose out of the exigencies of
war or the chase (for large game), or both, activities
largely not reducible to a prescribed routine—but origins
are problematic and not particularly to the point here. In
any case, human history has been in large part the story
of chequered relations between the members of this uneasy
partnership in interpreting and enforcing law. Treating

the law itself as eternal-and-immutable (divine or natural) seems to be implied in its being viewed as sacred.

An implication of unchanging law is that adult individuals will "naturally" know what the law is, largely without being aware of it as law, learning and even following it half-consciously, as they learn and use their language in accord with its laws. To the extent that they are aware of it as law, meaning that they feel it as compulsory, it becomes moral law, and still hardly presents an intellectual problem. In so far as conformity and obedience rest on fear of supernatural power, it may be called religious, or divine law, for which "natural law" is a terminological equivalent, historically implying ecclesiastical authority for declaring it. However, there can be no clear line between interpreting law and making law, whatever may be the pretensions of judges. And whatever may be or be supposed to be the source of law, it must always be what some legally constituted authority says it is—as long as it is effective as law, as long as it is not defied through rebellion, or changed to avoid this eventuality. Moreover, the same is the case with "truth," distinguished from private opinion, though in different fields the authorities attain to their position in diverse ways. In science the laws, or truths, are by definition found, not made, by those who declare them; but this is not strictly the case in fact. Even the "eternal and immutable" truths of religion have undergone much change—chiefly through the agency of prophets proclaiming a new revelation; but innovations have usually made way (when not suppressed) against the strenuous or violent opposition of the established priesthood, with the secular rulers taking one side or the other. With the revolution in culture that established liberalism—essentially rooted in the free pursuit of truth—this situation has been profoundly changed, in ways that will be sketched in the following and later lectures.

* * *

A basic fact, essential to any interpretation of modern society and its problems, is that any group must act through individuals as agents—at least any group of substantial size. The meaning of democracy is that the agents, the personnel of government, are held responsible to the society as a whole, and act by making and administering laws. Democratic political process is a mixture—rather inchoate—of choosing agents and prescribing within limits the nature of the laws, that is, defining more or less specifically the scope of the agents' discretionary powers. Ideally, the laws would express unanimous agreement, reached through free discussion; and ideally, they would not need literal enforcement. Unhappily, the first of these ideals cannot be realized, or closely approximated; and partly for that reason, partly because man is by nature a law-breaking animal (as well as a disagreeing one), the second also comes far short of realization in practice. In particular—for our purpose here—people often formally deny the axiomatic principle of mutual advantage in free exchange, or violate it when they formally accept it as valid. Much compulsion is necessary (to social order) in both interpreting and administering the laws. And further, laws must be made (changes introduced) because liberal society accepts the ideal of freedom-and-progress, which results in changes in both conditions and value norms. Hence action is required, through agents; and this creates a relation between rulers and ruled, which would be absent in ideal democracy; in that state the laws would be rules agreed upon by those living under them (the normal adults), embodying the terms of association.

All this applies to any "democratic" society, any community or group of free persons acting as a unit, in any field or any way. Government is the agency of group action, specifically that of formulating law, deciding questions left open by the inevitable vagueness of law, and settling disputes arising under the laws, private, public, and constitutional. The society of primary concern in these lectures is the sovereign territorial state assumed to be democratically organized. In the actual world, and for any future that is foreseeable or realistically conceiveable, a primary field of compulsorily unitary action is that of relations between a particular state and other states; but the problems of international relations can only be mentioned in these lectures. They will deal only with internal affairs, and chiefly with the problems set for the government of a state by "economic" affairs. That means action affecting the "economic order" which, along with the democratic political order, is the most conspicuous feature of liberal civilization. It operates through private property, prices of goods and services fixed in free markets, and free enterprise. These two freedoms, the economic and the political, plus the more fundamental intellectual and cultural freedom, are the three main aspects of individualism—as it is called, but for which "familism" would be a more descriptive name. Our concern is with the nature of intelligent public opinion as to the general social interest, which should guide action in the field indicated; but to establish and maintain such a public opinion is obviously the first task for political action, prior to implementing it. I shall not go into the detailed problems of governmental structure and operations, but the third and fourth lectures will essay a summary analysis of the economic order—as indicated in the general outline.

Social action is political action. In the economic sphere, its function is either to make the organization through markets and enterprise conform more closely to the pattern of individualistic freedom or to supplement this and remedy its defects, wherever improvement will result—important enough to justify coercion—or eventually to replace that system by having particular functions performed by governmental agencies. Any concrete issue calls for *comparing* the two systems of order in terms of consequences to be reasonably expected from each, appraised in terms of accepted social values. The supreme merit of the market-and-enterprise organization is that it embodies practically complete *freedom* —for the given individuals responsibly participating. The ideal market is completely free (with the qualification noted), since under perfect competition each party faces numerous equally good opportunities, so that no one has any arbitrary power over any other. There is no need for argeement, beyond accepting the axiom of mutual advantage in free exchange; each can follow his own desires, subject only to the free assent of the other party to any transaction. The situation is commonly described as "free competition," but rivalry as a motive has no rational place; it is antithetical to cooperation, and any "victory" is obviously cancelled by a defeat. The result of perfect competition is ideal cooperation, though the wish to benefit others is excluded from individualistic motivation, as well as that of obstructing their activities.

The competitive interest is also alien to rational behavior in politics, where in real life it plays a vastly greater role, and it is nearly universal in human social relations. This outstanding species of romanticism presents a major difficulty in the way of a rational approach to the analysis of social policy as well as in individual behavior. The difficulties are multiplied in the case of rivalry between groups—and most conflicts arise between groups, from families (the minimum effective social unit) up to national states, with innumerable group entities in between these, and beyond the state into alliances and blocs. They are further multiplied by organization for the sake of more effective rivalry, which is more or less true of organizations, in business and politics, and in general, notably in religion. Man is a social animal; human life is group life, and modern society has become an infinitely complex tissue of diverse and shifting groups, defying classification as to constitution and interests.

In contrast with the market, government (as already noted) inherently limits individual freedom by coercion. At the minimum a majority must "rule" one or more minorities, and the ideal of a majority decision on every issue can only be more or less approached in practice. Beyond this fact of majority dominance, further limitation on freedom are set by the inherent imperfection of the agency relation, which is ubiquitous in modern society and is of the essence of government. It is primarily a consequence of specialized knowledge and skill, and of the dynamic character of knowledge in particular. Decisions are constantly made by experts, on behalf of principals for whom they act by agreement. They must in large part judge the ends sought by those they serve, as well as the means for their realization, as there is never a clear line between the two. But even an individual principal cannot very rationally choose such an agent, or effectively hold him responsible, and it is vastly harder for a group.

Given freedom—possible freedom—the choice of the expert as agent becomes the concrete problem. This is notably the situation of the employee in a business enterprise in relation to the employer as his agent. For effective management, in the interest of the employee himself (as well as consumers and others) the employer must have power. Hence the freedom allowable to the employee is that of choosing among alternative employers. If market competition among employers is effective, any attempt to set up a power relation in the opposite direction will impair production, and can benefit employees only by violating the right to freedom of consumers, other employees, property owners, or entrepreneurs legitimately seeking gain—without which payment of wages is impossible. Only what a worker earns in a free market for labor is honestly called wages, and it is all that is his due from an employer as employer. These facts by no means dispose of the problem of income distribution as setting a task for government; they are intended only as a start toward indicating its nature—for further consideration (Lectures III and IV).

*   *   *

Since our problem is that of sound thinking (in a certain field), we must finally attempt a critical over-all view of human nature, the nature of the thinking and feeling mind. At this point I must comment briefly on man as a social animal. He is that, as the familiar adage says, but subject to conditions at least as important as the fact. He is also anti-social, the lawbreaker of the known world, rivalrous and a craver of power, so contentious that he often prefers victory to victuals. A member of groups in boundless complexity, he is predominantly social within a smaller group, especially when it is opposed by any other, and is inclined to rank his small-group interest ahead of the needs of a larger one including it—unless this is contending with another at the same level. Everybody believes in agreement and in cooperation, but this usually means that others should agree and cooperate with himself, and other groups with his own. Man is naturally a partisan and a gangster. It must be kept in mind that human nature evolved through the ages in small tribes, each in constant rivalry and potential or open conflict with its neighbors.

Tribal society was also static, and man evolved fearful of change and resenting it. Institutions and laws were religiously sanctioned; they showed little or no regard for justice, in the modern individualistic meaning; justice depended on inherited status. Karl Marx's view of religion as the opium of the people is fairly descriptive, but he ignored the difficulties of making any change for the better, without destroying the social order, the primary necessity. The religious attitude was functional, if not rational, in view of these difficulties and of men's basically romantic nature. The opium was necessary for survival, until and unless they should learn to discuss changes intelligently, and reach an improvement. This achievement is still largely in the future, and in doubt, particularly from the standpoint of economics, in view of the little visible headway so far made toward agreement on the meaning of distributive justice.

All problems of action are in large part problems of learning, hence, of education, either self-education or teaching-and-learning, and it commonly involves more or less un-learning. Problems of social action are educational, and that in a very broad sense. Human nature, intellectual and emotional, must be molded, in the individuals of each on-coming generation, to fit the environment, physical and social, as it is, as inherited from the past; and at the same time, must be equipped to improve it in both sectors. Human beings are born devoid of either conscious purpose or capacity for intelligent action—neither free nor fit for free-dom. In consequence, education is a *primary* task of adult society. For millions of years of social life, it presented no problem. In animal society the function was performed, in all needful aspects automatically, by the biological mecha-nism of instinct, with progress achieved by slow adaptation through evolution by mutations and selective survival. Through most of human history it was performed, still automatically in the main, by cultural inheritance; this also was subject to change, more or less adaptive, by a similar process, and by various historical forces, not to be discussed at this point. However, individual conduct departing from the established order, and any deliberate effort in that direction, were inhibited by the sanctification of custom and tradition, and institutionally ingrained fear of supernatural punishment for breaking any law.

In free and large-scale society, education becomes a social problem, because of the necessity for order of a large measure of like-mindedness, while the natural tendency of cultural drift is toward diversification—and because of the various romantic proclivities of what seems to be original human nature. The situation is one of striking historical novelty. The revolutionary conversion to liberal ideals of freedom and progress has largely removed the authoritarian religious and political brakes which until recently virtually suppressed the tendencies making for disunity and disintegration. The social task of education for fitness to promote progress under freedom while preserving tolerable order, is as hard as it is new. This is partly because the change has been so recent and sudden, in part because it is opposed by surviving ideas and feelings fitting men for life in the stationary society of past ages. The sanctity of the established naturally dies hard, and it is stoutly defended by powerful vested interests. At best, the religious attitude is slowly transferred to ideals of truth and right as subject to constant redefinition—if, indeed, the transfer is possible at all. Since freedom and all change conflict more or less with order, the primary essential, a delicate balance must be struck and maintained. Liberals tend to be romantically impatient for change and scornful of custom and habit, which must always furnish the main substance of order in social relations. They can be only slowly and gradually changed without destroying order or freedom, if not both. Human nature is also averse to the mental effort of critically considering the possibilities and costs of change, especially the labor of appraising alternatives and reaching intelligent agreement on what is desirable. There is an almost instinctive appeal to force, including persuasion, one of its most insidious and dangerous forms.

Much needful knowledge does not exist; but the primary lack is the inclination to use and seek knowledge, cooperatively, recognizing that it is chiefly a matter of judgment, not of crude fact or any simple formula. To live together in freedom, men must agree on the meaning of progress and on what can be done to promote progress. The former is the problem of ethics, as above defined; the latter involves all the sciences dealing with man, and especially an understanding of historical causality. In so far as ignorance prevails, in either of these fields—as it largely does in both—the course of change is better left to the "slow and silent forces" eloquently extolled by William James, that is, to the "natural" processes of history. Liberalism, so far from being the antithesis of conservatism, manifestly requires the latter as a counterpart. Lovers of freedom must resist the urge toward hasty recourse to compulsory legal and governmental action. Many evils and dangers must be tolerated in human life, and others met indirectly through the slow process of education, itself to be kept as free as possible. Democracy faces the hard problem of a proper division of functions between government and other forms of association, and policy needs to lean toward the more voluntary. The family heads the list, specifically in connection with education. And it is self-evident that with modern methods of preserving life, civilized standards are possible only if the natural birth-rate is restrained to keep numbers within the requisite relation to the means of support. About this problem little can be done by direct compulsion, for the most cherished and "sacred" of all freedoms is involved.

Chapter II ~ THE FREE SOCIETY: HISTORICAL BACKGROUND

In depicting the historical background of the free society, I must observe first that the main thing to be said is that history is just too much to know, to do anything with, and besides, history is not written in the way it should be written, for my purpose here. It is written largely as stories about the deeds of individuals, especially in politics and war, to the neglect of the other more fundamental things; these consist in the main of *fashions* that come and go. I take as the type the history of language—that is, history which nobody made. I want to stress the exaggerated idea we get in reading history about the extent to which men make history. History makes men, much more than men make history. Of course, there is no possible way to measure these variables and get a comparative evaluation.

Cultural history, in the general sense, is the thing that I should like to have and to promote, not to smother. I am not going to speculate about it because I am not able, but one thing that has struck me in trying to get at the historical background of liberalism (which I insist is a supremely important subject) is the peculiar periodization of the history of Western Europe. We had primitive society, classical civilization, and the Middle Ages—all of which could be further subdivided; and then we had the startling periods of change:

the Renaissance and the Enlightenment. Eastern Europe, and in particular Russia, did not have these stages. Russia took no interest in the Crusades and had no Renaissance or Enlightenment. Of course, Russian history was involved, in the first place, with the Byzantine tie-up and, in the second place, with the Mongol invasions. In any case, the epoch of liberalism of Western Europe is, I think, unique in fundamental respects. I would recommend one book to you if you are interested in history from the cultural point of view. The best thing I know—the best book of history and about history—is H. J. Muller's *The Uses of the Past*. He says the right things and says them in the right way—until he comes to talk about the profit system and the modern economy, where it is plain that he doesn't know what he is talking about.

Now, why do we talk about history? It is to help us understand the present and to look forward to the future. I have quoted Ortega y Gasset as saying: "Man . . . has no nature; what he has is . . . a history." His nature is, in a peculiar sense, a historical product, and, in an even more distinctive and extreme sense, the same is true for society. Certainly society has no original or general nature; it has a history. We know or infer the future only from the past. It is difficult enough to know the past—to know history— and harder still to learn from it. We need to know, however, something about historical causality—about the laws of history, in so far as it has laws—if we are going to make any intelligent plans for the future. This is terribly difficult, but we have to find the laws as best we can. We can act intelligently only in so far as we can distinguish between what is inevitable and what is more or less subject to human control. The difficulty is the main thing to be emphasized: the difficulty of learning history and of learning *from* history. Hegel, the great philosopher of history, said that what we learn from history is that men do not learn from history. (He could have left off the last "from history": what we learn from history is that men do not learn, "period"—from experience or otherwise; they are tragically inept about learning.) Another depressing thing is that the more obvious inferences from what we know about history have very somber implications for the enterprise of preserving and improving the kind of society to which we are committed: a free society.

These difficulties may be discouraging, but there is no point in living in a fool's paradise, or failing to see the problems that are there. I have to say that the problems are very difficult. History as a whole is against the possibility of a free society; it looks like a strange accident under a very peculiar concourse of circumstances that would not be likely to last very long. At least, to make it work is going to be a terrific task, but one which we have to attack and can only attack by attempting to understand it.

The supreme fact here is that the free society is a society with social problems. I said something about this in the last lecture: a democratic society is a society which, as a society, faces problems that have to be solved by its members acting collectively as a unit. And this is a very new thing in history. A great Liberal Revolution brought free society into the world, not overnight of course, but very suddenly in historical terms—in a small fraction of the thousandth part of the time the human race has lived on the earth. Normally man has lived under conditions which, in a broad general way, did not change in any essential—hardly any perceptible —degree. In this case, however, the basic conditions of life were turned upside down in just a few generations, and no more than a few generations ago. We have to date this inversion roughly from what is called the revolutionary period of the age of the Enlightenment in the later eighteenth century—the period of the American and French revolutions, and the founding of this American republic. The free society is a novel thing; and, as I said, it looks like a very strange product of a very strange concourse of circumstances.

Later I shall want to discuss other novelties in the course of history. There is, for example, the novelty of beings with problems of any kind, which the inert objects of nature, of course, do not have at all. Just where in the course of evolution do we encounter beings with problems? This question is a problem in itself.

History is important because—a theme I cannot develop— the problem of social action is to control the future course of history. Action is not taken merely to make repairs after mishaps or fatalities of one sort and another, such as economic depression, crimes, or even war. Action is taken to build a "higher" civilization. This is the fundamental objective, and on this the literature does not dwell. We talk a great deal about higher and lower civilizations, or more advanced or backward, but writers do not seem pushed seriously to say what they mean by higher civilization. I should almost say that if anyone has tried very seriously to describe a higher civilization, I haven't found it. I suppose a higher civilization is one which shows the greatest development and balance of all the fundamental values that enter into the "good life." But what are those values, and what do we mean by the best possible balance? These are questions I have not found anybody answering or trying to answer in a way that seems enlightening to me. Perhaps it is impossible, certainly it is very difficult.

I will remind you again that what has to be known in order to act intelligently by anybody in any condition is what *can* be done, the *consequences* of the possible courses of action (including not acting), and especially the *appraisal* of the results of different courses of acting or not acting. And I don't know which is the harder part: the prediction of the cause-and-effect sequence in relation to action, or the appraisal of values. The latter, in line with what I was just saying, is perhaps the more neglected. The problem is to state the meaning of "progress," because "progress" is our general objective, what we are trying to do, what we mean by improving society or civilization.

The task of government looks to the future. The responsible members of a society make up only about half the living population; we legislate and act for our children, and their children, for the unborn, not merely to adjust conflicts of interest existent at the given time. We must remember, too, that a society is acting upon itself. What do we mean by social free will? It has to have meaning, or else everything we say is nonsense. What we mean by social choice is a very much harder and more subtle problem philosophically than what we mean by individual free choice —which we have to assume to make any sense at all out of human action or conduct, even though the assumption is in conflict with postulates of the scientific world-view taken at all literally. These questions are very much harder than those in which an individual or group acts on the material world, where we have fairly definite scientific techniques with which we can predict the course of events in the absence of action and the results of action.

The need for action does not imply that society is sick. I get rather weary of the angry young men—willful, discontented, kicking, and grouching about the modern world, as if there had been a Golden Age not far back in history. Some of our books and periodicals are replete with this view. The point of view we have to take is that many problems are at most growing pains, and in general they do not imply anything wrong at all, but simply unrealized possibilities which have to be attacked in terms of understanding. We need a diagnosis of what is wrong in order to do anything about it, and to do this we have to know the case history. And in the case of society, the case history is simply history. The worst trouble again is not so much ignorance, but that people do not know they are ignorant; they know so much that is not true.

I need to go briefly into the general problem of history and science in relation to action. In a broad general way, history deals with the inevitable, and that is its function. Science deals with the hypothetically inevitable—what will happen if given conditions prevail or given things happen or are done. Functionally it deals with what is under control and with methods of control. I think that the sound view of the general relation between history and science from a methodological standpoint is the view associated with the names of Windelband and Rickert in Germany: that history deals with unique sequences, a unique nonrepetitive stream of events in time—that is, with "real" time; whereas science deals with the repetitive or constant aspects of a flow of events. But the relations are very complex. If we follow through with scientific explanation or causality, we should come out, of course, with an endless chain of causality that becomes a theory of history. But that result means a "block universe," which we know is unreal. We know the real universe has to have a place both for fixed predictable trends and for freedom or activity. The whole situation is full of paradox.

The great advance in modern times in the field of history has been the discovery of the principle of evolution, of continuous direct change in a more or less consistent direction in the cosmos, in biological life, and wherever we look for it. The principle was due to a bright idea which came to Charles Lyell and a few other people, primarily geologists to begin with: that conditions of the past could be explained by assuming that the same causes were at work throughout time as are at work now. Time and space are indifferent; under the same conditions the same thing happens wherever and whenever. That is the fundamental postulate of science, and one I have no disposition to quarrel with, if used with regard for its limitations—"chance" events and emergents in nature, and these plus creative freedom, in human conduct. I mention it here as bearing on the complex relation between history and science, between the continuously and inevitably evolving sequences of events and the more repetitive sequences, subject in general to some action by way of control.

In general, historical sciences are not useful: biological evolution, for example, is of no use to anybody except in explaining the phenomena. One cannot do anything with it. Modern science began with astronomy, the field in which there is least thought of trying to do anything about it. And I shall mention also linguistics, the most scientific of the disciplines dealing with human and social phenomena. The reason for this again is that we never think of doing anything about language. Language grows and changes;

but it is like what the scripture says about the wind: "It bloweth where it wisteth." We don't try to do anything about language, much as we should like to, and need to. We badly need a more rational method of communication, one that is more systematic and less ambiguous; and the world has got to the point where the need for a general language, at least an auxiliary lingua-franca, through which different cultures can inter-communicate with one another has become almost desperate.

So history is a chain of what we say is inevitable sequence. But, as a matter of fact, history is always producing novelties, and at relatively frequent junctures history produces startling innovations, revolutions, or what the most fact-facing school of evolutionists have called "emergents." I think we have to look at human phenomena, at human history, in terms of emergent evolution. New things come in, things that are not explicable, not predictable, in terms of what went before, and in general things that are categorically new do not replace the old but are superimposed on it. Thus, as evolution has progressed, the variety of subject matter has become more and more complex, particularly in the case of man. In that field of study we have to take a highly and irreducibly pluralistic point of view. Man is a physical-chemical mechanism and obeys the laws of physical process, as organisms have done since life appeared. And he has done so since the world was made, as far as we can measure in the laboratories of physics and chemistry. Man is also a biological organism and comes under the main principles of biology; he is in some respects a plant as well as an animal, but there are serious limits here. In addition, he has spiritual and mental qualities, partly conscious and partly unconscious, which make him a highly unique being in the universe. Only up to a point can we study man in the terms of physics and chemistry or even biology; much must be added, including many traits opposed to those of other animals.

One unique thing that man has is the capacity for history. There is a sense in which only man has a history; other things have a past, but not a history. Something new has come in with the advent of man: cultures, which, along with conscious mind, imagination, effort, will, and so forth, are not explicable at all in physical or biological terms.

One of our difficulties is that we know so little about the bare facts of the sequence of human evolution. Little can ever be known about human origins in particular; as we know little or nothing about the origin of life on the earth as a physical-chemical process, we know little more about the actual transition from animal to man. I read, not long ago, that all the intermediate primate bones that have been found and are supposed to shed any light on the evolution of man could be put in a fair-sized dresser drawer. And then what have you got? Fragments of bones. We will never know much about the acquisition of the qualities that make man human, that make him unique and worth study-ing, and a student of himself, his kind, and the world. We know that certain things happened, that man has some qualities that animals did not have, and that he got them somewhere and somehow in the course of the transition.

Here again I could find some fault with the study of human evolution. I understand the point of view of biologists and anthropologists as I understand that of the historians who write history the way they do: they write the history on which they can get the data, and the history that people want to read—both. People are fundamentally romantic; they want to read about the deeds of heroes. And the effort to delineate historical causality by historical laws would not be very popular even if it could be done much better than is actually possible. Biologists and anthropologists have studied the evolution of man chiefly in the terms in which they could get the data. They know a good deal more about the evolution of the skeleton than about anything else. From the few artifacts discovered, man has been defined as the tool-maker. But tool-making is only one of the distinctive characteristics of man; it is not at all certain that it was the first, even the first involving artifacts. Ornamentation and magical implements and practices, for example, may be as old, or older, but such articles would soon disappear and no record would survive.

We don't know the sequence in which social life developed in relation to animal life in general, or especially the connection in which government of conduct by intelligence was introduced. Moreover, the students of animal psychology have mostly either taken the mechanistic standpoint of behaviorism or at best have recognized mentality only as biologically instrumental reasoning. The neglect of the emotional side is puzzling, after Darwin set a good example, nearly a century ago. If there is one thing I want especially to stress, it is that this approach does not carry us far in talking about man. Most of the traits that are important for man and that are vital in connection with social problems are emotional and have little or no discoverable positive relation to biological utility. What good is a sense of humor or a sense of beauty? I could name a dozen traits that distinguish man and that have no explanation in terms of survival significance. Many are opposed; man sacrifices quantity of life for quality—which may be good or bad, in many senses of the words. Somewhere along the line

there has been a practical inversion of the instrumental relation between the mind and modern life. Unquestionably the
nervous system, the brain, and so forth, were once biological
organs functionally useful for the life of the organism and
the species. But civilized man thinks almost entirely in the
opposite way: biological life is instrumental to mental
experience of one kind or another, again, good or bad.
Man has often become ashamed of having a body at all, and
becomes addicted to mortifying the flesh and all that sort
of thing, thinking, talking and even acting in terms of a
war between the flesh and the spirit.

Particularly in the light of what biologists and anthropologists have studied and written we need to emphasize
the limitation of a biological approach to the study of man
and of human society. We do not know whether intelligence
—or, if we can distinguish it, instrumental intelligence—
arose first in non-social or in social species. There is no
proof as to whether man himself became first biologically
human or social, whether he rose out of a solitary or a social
ancestral species. For one thing, little is known about social
life among the higher subhuman primates. Man is always
referred to as a social animal, and all that is known certainly
is that he is a social animal now by preference as well as
by necessity, but apparently at least as much by necessity.
There are very strong indications that man was not originally and naturally a social animal, that he has been social-
ized by force, so to speak—by the force of biological necessity,
of biological utility, against his natural inclination. In any
case, there are other social animals, and there were social
animals, but without social problems, before man appeared,
and animals with problems but without society, long before
there was either man or society on the earth.

It is tempting to talk a little about the foolishness of some of the explanations historians have given for the origin of society. If there is any nonsense that surpasses the contract theory of the origin of human society, I should like to have an example of it. As a palpable fact, it is not society whose origin needs explaining as much as it is the individual. Human society is far older than the individual, in the sense of a member of an individualistic society. Modern society and the individual have evolved together, and men have become individualized in a way that, for instance, bees, termites, and members of other animal societies have not. Men have become individuals, in our sense, in the course of recent history—human nature and institutions evolving together.

Culture was the first great emergent on the way, definitely on the way, to man. Of course I mean culture as the biologists use the term, not "cultivation," or what the Germans call *Bildung*. It means patterns of behavior not inherited biologically through the genes but acquired by each new generation through imitation of their elders by the young. We know nothing of how this happened, or when. We cannot say whether men were men, in the sense of a biological classification, before they acquired culture or only after. There are traces, bare traces, of culture in some animals, particularly in some of the birds, whose young seem to learn by imitating the old, the old seeming in some way to encourage or teach the young. The otters teach their young to swim, and there are other similar cases. But in general, this type of permanence and persistence of behavior patterns that we call culture is distinctively characteristic of man. Such transmission of behavior patterns confers a very great biological advantage: and it does not necessarily imply intelligence or conscious life. It greatly increases flexibility and speed of adaptation, yielding what amounts to inheritance of acquired characters, that is, of learned behavior, a thing for which biologists have sought evidence. Physically, it would very greatly simplify the theory of evolution if we could believe in the inheritance of acquired character—as Lamarck and Darwin both did, as far as that is concerned. However, all the empirical and experimental evidence is against such inheritance, and the theory has been given up. But in the field of behavior, we get the same results through what I have been speaking of as culture.

With culture, history begins—history in a very unique sense, in the sense in which I said that only man has a history. Changes in culture are the subject matter of the kind of history I say we need in order to talk about the historical background of a liberal society; for all the great changes I am speaking about—in particular the liberal revolution of the Age of Enlightenment—are cultural changes. They are not events brought about by the planned action of anybody; they are of the nature of linguistic changes, changes that just happened, not because they were planned in any sense. One of the mysteries of culture is the infinite variety in which it has developed. When culture appeared, it differentiated; it seems to be the nature of culture to diverge.

We confront two mysteries here, equally mysterious as far as I can see. There is the unity of the human species biologically. The differences in the various so-called races of men are negligible. The innate physical differences that anybody can identify or to a degree measure are biologically unimportant, and no differences are discoverable in the humanly significant mental or spiritual traits. When culture comes along, it is exactly the opposite. It behaves much like Leacock's medieval horseman who rode off furiously in every direction. The model of cultural change is linguistic change, and there are thousands of languages, unrelated languages. Nobody can trace the history of the evolution of languages or know for certain whether they go back to any one common root. There are nearly a score of languages spoken in Mexico today as different from each other as Arabic is from English. One incidental mystery is that the languages of the New World—the languages of the original Americans, again meaning unrelated languages— are more numerous than those of all the rest of the world. This is true even though man's history does not go back very far in the New World. He certainly did not originate independently here, for none of the higher nonhuman primates are found anywhere in the Western hemisphere.

Man is the talking animal. Speech is purely cultural though presupposing adequate brain and nerve development. About the origin or the development of speech nothing is known. The mystery is that the most primitive languages known to students are often far more complex than the civilized languages. All known linguistic history is a process of devolution or disintegration, not of evolution; we can only guess as to how language was built up in the first place. It must have have been built up somehow from a simple means of expression in a fairly stable society to the complex systems we know, but this is one of those chapters of human evolution that we need and do not have, and probably have no way of finding out. Very much could be learned— especially in un-learning things that are not so—if people would think critically about language as a type of human conduct and of social process representing that element about which we can do nothing. I don't mean that absolutely, but so far the project has seemed hopeless and has hardly been seriously attempted. Quite a few people have invented artificial languages, but they haven't gotten anywhere with them, as we all know. And this is in the face of the great need we have for improvement in that regard. Speech is no proof of rationality. It is all right to treat speaking grammatically and coherently as an evidence of rationality when anyone is coming out from under an anesthetic or the like. But, in general, if you think of speech as indicating rationality, reflect on what people say, and then it looks different. What do they use language for, and what was language originally used for? I understand the balance of anthropological opinion to be that the original use of speech was to express and arouse emotion and not to communicate facts or reasoning: it was emotional, not intellectual.

One distinctive feature of man that must be stressed is art, the sense of beauty. Adornment may be older than tools for all we know; it is certainly very old. Most prehistoric artifacts show evidence of design for beauty, apart from instrumental, utilitarian significance. The designs have no biological value. One can invent ways of imputing biological value by postulating other conditions which would give such a value, but on the face of it the designs do not have it; the two aspects are rather negatively correlated. A curious thing as it seems to me is that men's sense of beauty, the world over and throughout time, as we know it— the human sense of beauty—is far more universal and common than men's sense of either right or truth. This was impressed on me first by the cave art of which we all have seen reproductions. The striking pictures painted perhaps twenty-five thousand or more years ago in the caves of France, Spain, and Northern Italy are the best known. I am told there are very similar things in the Southwestern United States that have not received as much publicity, although they would probably not be so old because the history of man in this part of the world does not go back so far. Anyway, those things are beautiful in our eyes. Much of the art of savage peoples all over the world is beautiful, whereas those people's ideas of what is either true or good would be simply weird, fantastic and often repulsive to our taste. This two-fold relation also holds between peoples of advanced culture; and there are signs of a kindred sense of beauty in some animals, notably species of birds.

Another curious thing is the relation between art and religion. Of course, religion is one of the explanations that have been invented for the cave art: people are supposed to have thought the pictures had magical power, that drawing pictures of animals would help bring them under control, help catch or kill them, or perhaps keep enemy species away. Well, maybe so. I don't see any way of knowing anything about it or much use in guessing; making hypotheses about the temporal sequence or causality where there is no evidence. A distinguished British art critic has argued that men communicated by drawing pictures even before they had speech, which would make art and a sense of beauty one of the very first marks of what is human. Much could be learned about man from reflection about beauty. The production and appreciation of beauty is a phase of human social life, interests, and conduct. It has impressed me that while all peoples think that their beliefs and their estab-

lished beliefs and ways of doing things are divinely com-
manded and ordained—are absolute, eternal, and immutable
—nobody has ever thought this about taste. The attributes
of deities, given infinite power and wisdom and goodness
and all that, do not include esthetic qualities or taste.

Man is certainly not the rational animal that he pretends
to be. He calls himself *homo sapiens* and doubtless thinks
it a compliment, though I do not know why it is even
that. He *is* very superior to other animals in reasoning power,
but reason is not distinctive of man and is hardly his
predominant trait; it is often used for irrational ends. His
feelings differentiate him more from the other animals and
are more important, particularly because his feelings furnish
the ends of action for which his reason supplies the means.
Man is no lover of truth as truth. He finds all sorts of fiction
much more interesting than truth: poetry, stories, myths,
jokes, wit, moral edification. New expressions of opinion
are very often interesting in proportion as they are unreasonable. Man is the opinionated animal. His main use
of reason is to find and give reasons for opinions reached on
other grounds. If we think about ordinary conversation
between people, what content does it usually have? What is
usually said? The most complimentary description is that
it is nothing. It is simply patter, self-expression, sociability.
Very largely it is an exchange in reverse: each one listens to
the other in exchange for being listened to. Man is a gram-
matic and superstitious animal, a contentious animal, a
competitive animal—which, by the way, is not the economic
motive. The economic motive excludes the motive of rivalry
and contention, although most economic activity is also
rivalrous and contentious. Political activity is more so. The

motive of rivalry and contention is as irrational in the one case as it is in the other.

The most primitive human society is very different from that of lower animals. Both have always obeyed law; everything in the universe obeys law—from atoms to planets— but they do not know they are obeying law. But man alone somehow became aware of obeying law, and he was against it. For many reasons he wanted to break the law, and he is the law-breaker of the universe. Man is not the social animal he pretends to be, either. He is unique in being antisocial, not in being social: he is the antisocial social animal. He is not only a law-breaker by nature, but is antisocial in other respects. Man belongs to infinitely many societies extending from his family and accidental conjunctions with friends and acquaintances, to his national status, usually to some group of allied nations, and finally the world. Within any group he is typically social when it is on the defensive against attack from the outside. When it is not, he is more or less antisocial. It is a sad truth that war makes men virtuous in the sense of courage and self-sacrifice within the group; but toward the enemy it converts human goodness into evil, and vice-versa. Man is by nature a patriot, a sectarian, and a gangster, and a selfish individual, but at the same time he has traits antithetical to all of these, and many more that are largely in pairs of opposites.

Do men love freedom or do they love power? They certainly love the freedom to get the power to be unequal, superior, in a way that limits freedom and would ultimately negate freedom. I think that is where a large part of the problem of free society arises. The evidence of human nature from folklore is as discouraging as that from history. From childhood I have thought about what awful things Grimm's fairy tales are: people seem to be naturally cruel, vengeful, and groveling. They want to pull down people from high places and put up others instead. It is only a question of who is to be "it." Laws have been enforced by fear, especially superstitious fear of supernatural punishment. Heaven has never been described as a democracy or a free private economy, competitive or cooperative. The human sense of social order has not been based on intelligence, but on force and fear, especially superstitious fear. Man lacks the elementary gumption to see that a society has to have rules, which means you keep the rules you have until you can get better ones. Instead of that, men will not obey the rules without some kind of compulsion; and evolution had to and did produce the superstitious fears that are the basis of social order in primitive society and very largely in civilized society—or at least people still pretend that they are. I become increasingly skeptical about that, but I don't know how to analyze such cases of historical and social psychological causality.

When Marx called religion the opium of the people, he did not recognize that the opium may be necessary. It is better to keep people from thinking until they can learn to think more or less correctly, which man does not do naturally; he prefers to think arbitrarily, romantically. The question on the knees of the gods today is whether people are acquiring or will acquire in time the capacity to think correctly enough to be able to maintain a free society without disintegration. Of course, innumerable civilizations have disintegrated before for one reason or another, but under conditions very different from those now prevalent.

Everyone will agree that man is a disagreeing animal.

How men have agreed even in small groups—how even tribes have come to have the same religion, the same correct usages, how they have even come to speak the same language—is a good deal of a mystery. Think of the geographical pattern of languages over the world and ask how or why it got that way. I do not see any general answer, except in using such words as "forces of history" and the like. Of course, in some cases one can find things that happened and acts by individuals that have made a difference in the persistence and change of culture. How did larger-scale societies get formed? Now we are in a world where we have to have a world society of some sort, better than we have, or be destroyed; there is no longer any argument about that. How have the world's societies expanded? By military conquest almost entirely. What is the chance of getting a world society by intelligent discussion and rational agreement? Well, we have to work at it and try to have faith that, if we make headway, time will be on our side and we can finally work things out.

It is clear that a crucial part of the world situation, this world crisis we hear so much about, is that human nature simply has not evolved in or by or for this kind of world, this kind of social environment—a world of large-scale, free, mobile, progressive, rationalistic, individualistic relationships. In so far as men are, or could be assumed to be, rational animals, the great problem of history would be to explain decadence. Why have civilizations decayed and gone to pieces? Decadence is written all over the face of history, and I do not think it is difficult to see why. When there gets to be anything at all worth quarreling about, people begin to quarrel, and then go to fighting over the division of the benefits of culture, instead of working to maintain or develop it. In that respect, our society is moving into the same situation others have found themselves in, the situation described, which probably explains the phenomenon of decadence more than any other one thing.

The towering example of decadence in history is, in my point of view here and now, the decline and fall of classical civilization—what Gibbon called the triumph of barbarism and religion. This might be hyphenated: barbarism-and-religion. The connection certainly holds in one direction: barbarian societies are always religious. Whether it holds in the other way—whether religious societies are necessarily barbarous, and civilized necessarily secular—cannot be asserted or denied. But the fact is plain that the classical cultures were predominantly secular. Religious authority prevailed chiefly in ecclesiastical affairs. This was changed when the ancient world was converted to what was called Christianity—modeled on the decadent Empire itself and more correctly described as "churchanity," it bore little relation to the teachings of Jesus and Paul, the historical founders of the religion. The religious order came to dominate, and there was a reversion to barbarism, to extreme primitivism, in essential respects. For the main purposes of our topic—the historical background of liberalism—we do not need to go further back than the Middle Ages. We can consider the evolution of liberalism out of conditions then prevailing as representing in epitome the whole course of evolution from primitivism. Of course, there was the so-called Renaissance, which was a real rebirth to some extent. It was a resurgence of civilization, and it was influenced by the rediscovery of classical art and thought. But I think the element of rediscovery is very much exaggerated. The new civilization was very different from the old and was created fundamentally by forces quite different from the dissemination of the old manuscripts after the fall of Constantinople in either 1204 or 1453, to which we usually impute the beginning of the Renaissance. Some of these forces will be noticed presently.

As to the primitiveness of medieval society, Henry Osborn Taylor has written two interesting volumes about the medieval mind. It's interesting to read what people in that age believed about biology and its symbolism. The unicorn and the phoenix and other weird animals taught very edifying lessons about the church, and the virgin, and the Holy Ghost, and so forth. When Galileo made a telescope and discovered the satellites of Jupiter and published the fact, he was met by the following argument of the head professor of philosophy in the University of Padua. Galileo called these satellites the Medicean stars, and the professor proved that such objects do not exist. We know, he said, that there are seven planets and only seven, because there are seven openings in the human head to let in the light and the air: two eyes, two ears, two nostrils, and a mouth. And the seven metals and various other examples also show that there have to be seven. Besides, the stars are invisible to the naked eye; therefore, they do not influence human events: therefore, they are useless; therefore, they do not exist (*Quod erat demonstrandum!*). That was in 1610, which is supposed to be well out of the Middle Ages, far along in the Renaissance.

I have some ideas, more or less speculative (which is true of everybody's ideas about historic causality), about what gave rise to a resurgence of civilization and the development of a new kind of civilization. Starting with the ecclesiastical authoritarianism of the Middle Ages, one thing that I have not been able to find discussed in history to my satisfaction, is religious persecution. As far as I know, torture for heresy is practically a monopoly of Western Christendom and specifically the Roman Catholic Church. It quickly died out after the Reformation. Religious intolerance is distinctive of the Semitic group: Judaism, Christianity, and Islam. Outside of medieval West-European Christendom there has been little torture, though there have been some executions for heresy. One part of the problem is that the tie-up between church and state makes it hard to distinguish between heresy and treason. But there is no question about the burning alive for religious heresy by the Holy Inquisition, Spanish and Roman, as intellectual independence revived after the long medieval night of scholasticism and enforced dogma. Ten years before the incident with Galileo just cited, Giordano Bruno was publicly burned at the stake in Rome for trying to talk a little sense about the solar system, along similar lines with what Galileo did, and criticizing the Church along Reformist lines, and Galileo was presently forced to recant and spent his last years under arrest. Of course, the Church in the Middle Ages always said that it only controlled faith and morals—that is, only what people thought and what they did; apart from that, they had complete liberty.

I think that the growth of heresies had a great deal to do with putting an end to the Middle Ages. They were not movements for freedom and progress, but called for restoring something like original Christianity in place of the pretenses and unscriptural practices of the Church. The main official orthodox doctrines had no substantial connection with the teaching of the founders of Christianity according to the accepted records, the only evidence in existence, and the Church officialdom was corrupted by wealth and power. Protestantism—the Reformation, so-called—was simply the first one of a succession of heretical movements that got enough political power behind it to resist extermination. It fought for a century and a half one of the most terrible series of wars in history, the so-called Wars of Religion, in which other interests more and more predominated from the start and which finally merged into a struggle between religion in general and the new learning of scholarship and science.

The change from medievalism to modernism occurred in two stages. The first one, the period of the Renaissance and Reformation, was not a liberalizing movement. Politically, it was rather the contrary; it increased authoritarianism. What it signified was the transfer of authority from the Church to the new states. The development of these new national, monarchical states—which were just as absolutist in theory as the Church had ever been, and in some ways more absolutist in practice—led to liberalism for two reasons. In the first place, the dominance of the political state over the ecclesiastical order was fundamental, as I said was true in Greece and Rome. Political power has never been as opposed to change, as dogmatic, as the ecclesiastical order. It has been more disposed to be reasonable and to adapt means for the achievement of ends. In the second place, the development was in the form of a plurality of national states, in a diplomatic and military competition with each other that had already been going on for centuries and that necessarily involved development of trade and science. These latter were the main real ferments of the change, as I see it. The new states had to encourage both trade and science, which seem to be inherently individualistic, because they were the main source of new wealth; and new wealth was the sinews of war. Again war, and not discussion—not any innate predilections of the human race for freedom and rationality—was what dominated the sequence of change.

A lot of things happened. One of the very interesting things in the late Middle Ages was the importation of techniques which had been used in the East, based on empirical craftsmanship rather than science. These techniques played a tremendous role in the West. The Chinese had had both gun powder and printing on paper, many centuries before they were introduced in the West. They knew about the lodestone but had not used it as a compass. The first great technical innovation, and the most important, was the Arabian mathematics, specifically the columnar notation. This made computation possible for the common man and mathematical ideas a part of general education. The Arabs had got it from the Hindus, but neither of these peoples had used it in business (accounting) or in science. Manifestly, neither of these activities as we know them, could get along without arithmetic—and the elements of algebra were introduced with it, early in the thirteenth century. It is a curious fact that the Maya Indians of Guatemala and Yucatan had used a columnar notation early in the Christian Era, a millennium before Columbus. Detailed differences are that their columns were horizontal, and the value ratio was 20 instead of 10. All this was of course unknown in Europe, but many essentials of the new technology were old in parts of Asia, while Europe was slow in following the example. Both printing and paper were in use in Persia in the eleventh and twelfth centuries—spread from China by the Arabs, and other traders who were moving back and forth across the land. Paper is historically the more important; if an abundant and cheap writing material had been available, printing would no doubt have developed long before it did. It is controversial how far several of the new techniques were rediscovered, how far introduced from the East.

A peculiarity of the new scientific movement was its close relation to practical applications, which was not the case in ancient times. There was then a social chasm between aristocratic philosophical circles and the vulgar craftsmen. At the same time, West-European culture developed a new interest in knowledge for its own sake. The first field of such curiosity was geography—following upon the Crusades —which grew out of pilgrimages. This was soon followed by astronomy, badly needed for navigation, in turn important in exploration and hence for trade—but it was also tied in with a complex romantic interest in the stars and astrological beliefs. There is a mixture of utilitarian motives with more or less scientific curiosity and a sheer love of adventure and even the propensity for gambling. On the side of method, a new empiricism teamed up with a revived interest in mathematics—shown in astronomy by Copernicus, and strikingly by the relation between Tycho Brahe and Johannes Kepler—in whom the mathematical interest had a mystical and theological tinge—and again in Galileo. In the time of Copernicus the Italians were making great advances in mathematics, and modern anatomy was born, in a book by Vesalius, the same year that saw the posthumous publication of Copernicus' work.

The scientific importance of all this is fairly familiar, less so is the more important fact that the "Copernican Revolution," probably effected in reality by Galileo, marked a cultural revolution. The new picture of the solar system might almost be called negligible in comparison with the radical change in the conception of Truth itself. The previous idea that all humanly relevant knowledge had been given once and for all, by revelation, gave place to the antithetical view of it as progressive, subject to constant revision, through *free* investigation, discussion, and publication. It was a long step from burning Giordano Bruno alive in Rome in 1600, for expressing a somewhat objective interest, to the mere silencing of Galileo when, just a few years later, he effectually launched the revolution with his telescopic discovery of the satellites of Jupiter (the "Medicean Stars") and with other visible facts in contradiction with Genesis and Aristotle. Theological opposition of course subsided slowly; the battle for intellectual freedom started over in the later nineteenth century, with the promulgation of the theory of evolution by Darwin and Wallace—and is still not entirely won.

The scientific revolution in world-view was only a quite indirect result of the Renaissance, and the modern conception of man and society—more important for our purpose—is still more remotely connected. This revolution followed slowly upon the former, and developed in Northern Europe, through a different sequence of historical causality. The first stage, as already noted, was the displacement of the Church as the supreme authority by "the State." But as this meant new national states, under dynasties ruling by divine right, essentials were little affected. The states themselves were produced by concentration of feudal power in the hands of territorial princes, who became absolute monarchs. In the early seventeenth century, Francis Bacon preached the gospel of progress in the form of increasing mastery over nature through inductive science, and sketched a Utopia built around this central idea. The century was almost as remarkable for the promulgation of such schemes as it was for the revolutionary scientific advance, and the final phase of the Wars of Religion. However, ideas of liberty or political democracy—or even religious toleration—were far from the minds of the leaders of thought, though Deism and natural-theology represented progress toward rationalism, which became ascendent in the Enlightenment, particularly in France, in the later eighteenth century. The great final result was "liberation of the mind" (J. B. Bury's expression) from dictatorship, ecclesiastical or political. On this followed the democratization of the monarchy, primarily in Britain, beginning with the victory of Parliament over Stuart absolutism, late in the seventeenth century. In this achievement the British colonies in North America played a vital role, for their War of Independence led to the French Revolution. The movement went on through the nineteenth century and beyond, with gradual extension of the suffrage, until the sex qualification in politics was abolished, in the leading Western nations, after the first World War.

Parallel to the democratization of politics, and inseparably connected with it, went the liberation of economic life (*laisser faire*) under the leadership of Adam Smith and his followers, the classical economists. They were largely the same persons as the Utilitarians in moral philosophy, followers of Jeremy Bentham, who began serious publication in 1776, the date of Smith's chief work, *The Wealth of Nations*. (Also the year of the American Declaration of Independence, over a year after the beginning of the Revolutionary War.) The phrase, *laisser faire,* refers to the freeing from the "shackles" of state control (that of the Church was already in the past) of the "economic order" of exchange in open markets and private enterprise. The extremes of economic individualism led to a reaction in Britain, after which the relations between the progressively democratized state and this economic system came to be the central problem calling for intelligent social action. The quest for rational norms is its primary intellectual phase; but prior to that is the will to be objective, in questions asked and answers sought. How repugnant this attitude is to human nature is the great lesson of history. The progress of natural science has made it hard for us to realize the kind of thinking that previously prevailed. At the time of Tycho Brahe, in Galileo's earlier life, the medieval view of comets was still accepted—that they were formed by the ascending from the earth of human sins, formed in a kind of gas, and ignited by the anger of God. This poison then fell on people's heads, causing all kinds of evils, from bad weather to pestilence. In politics, however, no such progress has yet been achieved. Much that passes for argument today in that field, and in business relations, if less crudely superstitious, is the sales-talk, propaganda; it is not much more realistic or sound. But it is no doubt what is effective, in the main; natural selection must result in the survival of the fittest, in that sense.

Chapter III ~ THE ECONOMIC
ORDER: STRUCTURE

In the last lecture I distinguished the development of two
social orders as a result of the liberal revolution, of which
the industrial revolution was an important part. The reality
of the latter has been called into question by some historians,
but I think we are still justified in using the expression
"industrial revolution," knowing that what we mean is
primarily a technological revolution, but radical change in
the social-economic order was involved as both cause and
effect. In the later eighteenth century and the early nineteenth century society developed into two fairly separate
orders, which I called the political order and the economic
order. Cultural and other social relations are to some extent
independent of both, but these phenomena are not in point
here. They too were phases of the same movement, and I
do not think we could have ever had our democratic, free
political order without that of free enterprise, but that is
not a problem to go into here. These two orders involve
two kinds of men—the political man and the economic
man—who inhabit the same skin along with quite a number
of other men of different kinds, largely incompatible, yet
coexisting, and none of them to be ignored in the discussion
of society and its problems. Both of these orders—the political
order and the economic order, form the subject matter of

new sciences; we have the politics or political science of democracy and the economics of free enterprise; and each is in a way a part of the other. The economic order in an inclusive sense clearly includes the political and also constitutes one of the main fields of its activities and problems.

The term "free enterprise" is used for lack of a better one. This seems to be the best description, or the least question-begging; any name is objectionable as prejudicial for or against, and most of them are in dispute. The term "capitalism" was introduced by Karl Marx as a condemnatory epithet and is most undescriptive. It was coined and disseminated to imply that capital employs labor—and, of course, bosses, dominates and exploits labor. In a correct view of the system a third party, the entrepreneur, hires both of them, which places the capitalist and the laborer in the same position in the organization. The real capitalist is the money lender, the third party, the entrepreneur. As to that confusion, however, I must say for Marx that he only copied the fallacy—as he did most of his other main dogmas, particularly the worst of them—from the classical economists. In general and socially speaking, that is, in terms of the instrumental point of view, the political order has, along with other functions, its major role of solving problems that arise in the economic order. Regulation of the latter has come to be much the most controversial and important field for state activity, the function that bulks largest and creates the most controversial issues.

This functional view itself raises methodological issues that tend to distract from what may superficially seem to be the main substance of our topic. It implies that the economic order has knowable, predictable ways of behaving —a persistence underlying change, nothing unchanging unless acted on by some outside force, but that the political order can interfere with its natural tendencies and redirect them. Then the political order must belong to a very different category of being. It must be an entity with will and intelligence and purposive capacities. If we look at politics as a controlling agent and economics as subject to control, the one acting and the other passive, they are seen to belong to different philosophical categories.

That economics can then be a science while politics cannot be, states a contrast that is valid, but only up to a point; its truth is limited on both sides. The sense in which either study is scientific would need lengthy interpretation. The field of methodology is tempting, hard—at least for one with my temperament—not to get into, and harder still to get out of in any reasonable length of time, without getting bogged down in what appears to most people mere verbiage. Yet it seems to me to include a good deal of what the citizen needs to know to be intelligent and educated and competent for his role. The general repugnance to methodology, to clarifying basic concepts is one of the main obstacles that economics, and especially political economy, has to face. It obstructs the general acceptance of economic truisms which the public needs to grasp, both for the sake of understanding and to have knowledge required for practical use in solving social problems.

While there is a contrast between politics and economics, in this regard, both have an objective side—scientific in the sense of being impersonally objective, describing a kind of reality different from what people wish were true, or think ought to be true. But along with their scientific character, both have other sides. They both deal with the conduct of and decisions expressing the mentality of the same human beings, for membership in both orders is, of course, identical. And these people exemplify many kinds of entity. They are mechanisms in which the laws of physics and chemistry hold good, animal organisms, and also individuals more or less free and intelligent. On top of that they are, to a considerable extent, romantic, capricious, exploratory, and unpredictable. In a full discussion of these problems, one would have to go into a general treatise on human nature —into psychology, anthropology, sociology, and so forth. These fields are scientific in some senses and degrees, along with physics, chemistry, and physiology, which are admittedly scientific. But physics and chemistry tell us little about human nature, and scientific biology not a great deal.

So one must ask, what do we mean by "science," anyway? The structure of the economic order is the main subject matter of economics, and economics calls itself a science. In English at the present time, the word "science" has come to mean primarily not knowledge in general but natural science, positive, empirical, and analytical, and economics is held to be a science on the model of the natural sciences. In what sense or how far this type of science can apply in treating of man, especially modern civilized man, who has all the other characteristics going with freedom— romantic predilections, the experimental attitude, and so forth—that is a question to be faced before one can understand, or adequately analyze, the main subject matter of economics and politics. Natural sciences are regularly described in terms of the function of prediction and control— or of prediction alone in adaptive behavior where control is not in question, as in sciences like astronomy and meteorology, and also human anatomy and physiology. Incidentally, modern science began at almost exactly the same moment in the two general fields, nature and man. Copernicus' book on the revolutions in the heavens and that of Vesalius' on human anatomy, the first approach to that subject from the empirical point of view, were both published in the year 1543. (Anatomy of course is a physical science.) At that time and in those fields I would say that intellectual freedom as well as modern science should be said to begin; it is a very important date in history, which one ought to remember.

I must say, dogmatically if you like, that prediction or control, or both, do not and cannot apply in a literal sense to social science; that is, knowledge cannot be used in social science in anything like the same way as in man's dealings with natural objects. This is one of the great difficulties. Science in this sense—knowledge used for prediction and control—simply does not apply in a society with freedom and equality. I take it as self-evident that one does not know oneself in the main through sense observation and induction, nor control oneself by manipulation of matter, which is the only way in which man has any control over nature. Nor does one person know others primarily by observation and induction, nor control others by literal manipulation. These statements are argued vehemently back and forth, and round and round; but I submit them all the same as self-evident. One both knows and influences others primarily by meaningful intercommunication, which we do not have with natural objects and which they do not have with each other. It is essentially a mutual relation, where that of men to nature is unidirectional. Physical objects do not know or use men, or strive to do so. I pass over the relations between men and the higher animals.

Prediction and control between human beings obviously cannot be mutual—two cannot predict and control each other at the same time—and free society must exclude unilateral control. For one person to control another in a one-sided way is the antithesis of freedom, and we are postulating free society as both a reality in part and the ideal to which we are committed. Scientific method in the sense of being useful for prediction and control has meaning in human society only for an absolute dictator. If one can imagine a dictator who really owned his subjects and had absolute authority over them, he would be in a position, assuming a wish to do so, to treat them as one treats machines. Even then there would be very serious limitations because after all most people do have minds and feelings and wills and that sort of thing, and they make a lot of difference. People can be ruled, as the saying goes, mostly by fooling them, and we do not control natural objects that way or by any process of coercion. Coercion has no meaning in that context, as only a free being can coerce or be coerced; but freedom and coercion are the main facts in social relations.

At this point something should be said about the real nature of what is called "social control." The phrase is largely a misuse of words if it is thought of in terms of science and technology, that is, what the words mean literally. What is referred to is the procedure by which a society maintains or changes itself. It is not control but a process of reaching collective decisions, a consensus, which is a totally different kind of thing. Now in reality, the same people who are regulated, by acting politically through law and administration as a unitary group, control—or, as we say, rule—themselves in their capacity of acting individually. More specifically, in their capacity of acting economically, which is a particular and very special mode of acting, not to be

confused with other kinds that also come under the purview
of the political control process. Yet the various modes of
acting by man are not in the main separable. It is not a
matter of distinguishing classes of cases in which people
act one way or another. They act in many of the ways in
nearly any act, and these different types of action—economic
behavior, criminal behavior, social behavior, esthetic behavior, one cannot even make an exhaustive list of them—
are aspects or elements in conduct which enter into any
particular choice of behavior in different proportions and
in different ways and make the whole problem of analysis
extremely difficult, and far from definite and objective even
when you carry it as far as you can.

The task of economics as a discipline and as a branch
of knowledge is to describe the structure and functioning
of the economy, of the modern Western type, a free economy
with markets and prices and private enterprise. But it is
descriptive only in so far as the economy is made up of
individuals who behave economically, i.e., are "economic
men." The concept of the economic man is valid and useful;
it is fundamentally true that men behave economically,
that is, as economic men, to an important degree. But also
to a large extent they do not; their motivation is mixed;
they behave in many other ways, even in part at the same
time. The economic view of man is far from being the
whole human reality, or even an accurate description where
it is valid as a partial, abstract view. This and other features
of more or less economic behavior are more or less contra-
dictory. People often behave romantically, in one or another
of many senses, which is in principle the opposite of behaving
with economic rationality; it covers the poetic, humorous,
or disgusting, the feelings side of life. Yet one may rationally

economize means in pursuing a romantic objective. And behaving economically tells little about what anyone is actually doing—*what* means are being used effectively, to *what* end.

The statement that economics describes the way the economic order works refers to its working as a mechanism; that is the meaning of being scientific. But here we encounter a paradox: If one behaves with perfect economic rationality he does not behave rationally as a human being. At the limit, instrumental rationality runs over into the very different category of mechanistic cause and effect. It would be irrational to be, or try to be, perfectly rational; this is the verdict of common sense. Analysis must simply ignore this element of self-contradiction and use the concept of complete rationality—the economic man—which is anyhow far more unrealistic in other respects. Philosophically, as well as for common sense, rationality implies some chance of error and some actual error. Realistically, of course, people's thoughts and conduct are full of error and at least two other deviations from perfect rationality that are worse. The first is ignorance—being oblivious of a question that conduct must somehow answer is not the same thing as making a wrong judgment. And still worse is prejudice, a hydra-headed monster—"knowin' so derned much that ain't so." Objectively defined, prejudice and romanticism are near synonyms, and the line between either and a rational (that is, intelligently critical) value judgment can never be clear. For the economic man all interests in or involving other people, except only a purely instrumental interest, are irrational, romantic; they include both cooperation and competition (rivalry) as motives, and of course all loyalty to persons, groups, or causes. Rivalry is the worst "corruption," especially as, coupled with loyalty, it is the main ingredient in nationalism. Another is the exploratory interest—seeking answers to questions, answers which are not expected to be of any "use" when found. All these interfere to prevent perfectly rational behavior, equivalent to mechanical response, though perhaps we can conceive of the subjects being consciously aware of it, in a completely passive way.

Exchange between perfectly rational beings can be visualized only if they operate through vending machines and no one knows anything about his opposite number in any transaction. Even then we would have to use the abstraction of a "perfect market."

These observations suggest another difficulty. Natural science deals with phenomena that are not affected by the prejudices or wishes of the investigator nor by the publication of the results of his investigation, which is more important (except indirectly as a law is found and used by man to direct his manipulative behavior and so change the course of natural events). The phenomena observed by the natural scientist are not influenced by any form of persuasion or suggestion, as is so markedly the case with human conduct in society. (Recent developments in physics have shown that they are influenced by being observed, but outside the field of electronics the effect is negligible.)

If we could write economics as observed from some other planet and if we never published the results on earth, economics would come nearer to being a natural science. But it would still not be a science in the empirical sense in which physics and chemistry are sciences; for it deals with motivated behavior and motives are not observed by the senses, and it is affected by error. Further difficulty in expounding any knowledge about society is that it is practically impossible for the writer or speaker himself to suppress approval and disapproval or avoid language which indicates or suggests his own likes and dislikes—which again the investigator does not feel towards physical phenomena. He does not care how they work, but only seeks to find out and explain. But the man who is writing about social phenomena does care, and it becomes very difficult, if not impossible, to keep his caring out of his exposition, or suppress all effort to influence. Of course that is what social science is intended to do, in large part, in spite of pretenses to the contrary. It is no marvel that the classical economists were accused of being apologists. I suppose three quarters of the economists writing today accuse each other of being special pleaders for one interest or another—and this is more or less true, with the possible exception of the mathematical economists. Such things keep economics from being very strictly scientific. It has been called the "dismal science" by Carlyle, and others who didn't know what they were talking about, because it teaches that social measures do not necessarily have only wished-for consequences. People's interests in social phenomena differ from their interests in natural events in another respect. In social phenomena we deal with a particular unit of some kind, a more or less unique individual, and not with huge quantities, numbers, and classes of a uniform description, as in the case of the atoms and the causal sequences which make up the physical world.

The basic structure of the economic order is not terribly complex if one does not go too far into factual details. The difficulty of getting it understood is partly repugnance for abstract thinking but in a greater degree it is moralistic prejudice. I find it useful to approach this task in terms of a fourfold division of the subject matter—a cross-dichotomy

—and to develop it by proceeding from the simpler aspects to the more complex, from greater to lesser abstraction and generality, and so build up towards reality. But no theoretical or explanatory science can ever be very realistic. Although theoretical mechanics is about as unrealistic as analytical economics, people seem to have natural sense enough not to apply the principles of frictionless machines without making the necessary qualifications and without getting by experiment the necessary empirical and quantitative data in addition to the abstract principles. The two fields are more or less parallel in this respect, but people want to throw economics out because it is unrealistic, while they go ahead and use physical engineering more or less intelligently, although the unreality is not very different, but in fact it is the engineers who do that; the public accepts the results without needing or in general much caring to understand how they are achieved. In economics it is different, for reasons partly not too obscure, but which cannot be discussed here.

Now to get on with the fourfold scheme. First, there is a main division between individual and socially organized economic behavior. I have been talking about the former, pointing out some philosophical problems. Then we must consider individual economic behavior—and later the socially organized—first with respect to conditions which are given in certain fundamental respects, chiefly as behavior which uses given means to achieve given ends, and secondly with respect to the use of means to produce more means in order to improve the individual's condition instead of going on at a uniform level. The second main category, associative action, or organization of economic activity through markets, must be considered under the same two divisional heads, along with complications of social life.

For handling the first part of the first main division—

individual behavior under "given" conditions, the concept of a Crusoe economy seems to me almost indispensable. This has come to be another cuss-word to people who crave realism and are contemptuous of theory, largely because they uncritically dislike the individualistic economy. I do not see how we can talk sense about economics without considering the economic behavior of an isolated individual. Only in that way can we expect to get rid by abstraction of all the social relations, mutual persuasion, personal antipathies, and consciously competitive or cooperative relationships which keep the behavior of an individual in society from being, in any closely literal sense, economically rational. Crusoe would be in this position: he would actually use given means to achieve given ends, his purely individualistic wants. Under the given means I include, somewhat arbitrarily, a given technological knowledge, and know how, as well as our subject's personal capacities, physical and mental, and all external instrumentalities under his control. Whenever he gets new technological knowledge, he is increasing his economic resources. But in saying that he is using given means, I do not assume that the concrete instruments are naturally everlasting. I assume that some at least are subject to wear and tear or depletion, and hence must be maintained or replaced, but that this is done in such a way as to keep the total at a constant or stationary level. Crusoe must maintain his productive capacity, which includes repairing and replacing anything that is used up or worn out. That is necessary to avoid consuming out of capital and maintaining a constant level of consumption itself. The treatment of one's own person as a productive instrument is obviously correct. But the procedure involves serious difficulties; chiefly that the maintenance of the productive instrument in this case cannot be separated from the subject's consumption, which is an end, not a means. His ordinary consumption both maintains him as a productive instrument and gives him satisfaction, which is the purpose of all his activities. We get an overlapping of means and ends that is a source of difficulty for any sharp analysis. Some of the classical economists, notably John Stuart Mill, thought that it is possible to distinguish between the cost of maintaining a laborer and the consumption of the laborer as something additional, which alone yields pleasure or satisfaction. He used the terms "productive" and "unproductive consumption" to differentiate the two. This amounts to assuming a zero point at which consumption as satisfaction would begin. He thought of the amount and level of consumption up to a certain level as merely maintaining the worker in a neutral mental state, and only beyond that becoming consumption in the sense of a good or end. This would be the point at which life would be barely worth living, perhaps a suicide point, for completely rational behavior. To my mind this is one conceptual separation that is so unrealistic that I would not use it, although it is more or less real, and the vagueness of many distinctions that have to be drawn is an unescapable feature of our analysis and exposition. The maintenance of physical capital without quantitative increase or decrease also involves some "unrealism."

The economic problem of Crusoe is to apportion his different productive resources among different uses, different modes of satisfaction and different products—assuming stationary conditions. There is one correct apportionment, that is, one that provides more satisfaction than any other. This maximum is defined on the basis of the marginal principle, the principle of diminishing marginal utility and equalization at the margin. Resources are obviously apportioned incorrectly between any two uses if the subject gets a larger final increment of satisfaction from the same increment of any resource in one use than the other. The modern economists—the bright young men in the profession who are devotees of mathematics and formal logic—have been quarreling of late about the principle of diminishing utility, and it has been thrown out of a number of books, even elementary textbooks. To my mind there are problems here about the kind of quantity a level of satisfaction is—real problems—but I don't see any sensible argument against treating satisfaction as a quantity in the ordinary cardinal sense. We can and do compare additional, alternative increments of different things and on that basis make decisions. One assumes that the economic subject, the isolated Crusoe, has several kinds of resources and knows about various products and kinds of satisfaction that these resources can be used to yield. His problem is to apportion his resources among these uses and combine them in each use in such a way that satisfaction is maximized. When all resources taken individually are correctly apportioned, they are also correctly proportioned or combined; our textbooks do not make this as clear as they might.

The second step would be to consider a Crusoe who is using some of his resources to "improve his condition," a purpose to which Adam Smith thought every man devotes a uniform, constant, and uninterrupted effort. Of course, this is nonsense: any considerable effort to "get ahead" characterizes relatively few, even of Scotsmen, and even in Adam Smith's day it was a very new thing in history, and is not at all generally characteristic of the human race even

yet. Most people are content to live at a stationary level, if
they have reasonable confidence in its remaining stationary,
that is, not deteriorating noticeably. In any case, this improving of conditions occurs in our society; it is achieved
by the economic activity of saving and investment. An
increase of resources comes about through sacrificing current
consumption and using resources that could have been used
for that purpose to produce means for increased consumption
in the future. The question arises whether there is any
rational principle of marginal equalization between current
use and provision for the future, any that stands on something like the same level as the principle of marginal
equalization of utilities in the stationary economy. It is
a very different kind of a problem; such a principle is
logically implied in the choices people make, but its validity
is a question to which I do not know the answer. There
probably is no definitive answer. When the present is being
compared with the future, the latter means the indefinite
future, and a comparison cannot be made very rationally.
In making these decisions, people are certainly looking
beyond their own lifetimes even if they do not so wish or
intend. Of course, they usually do so, to some extent, to
provide for heirs or leave an estate. But, even if they did
not, most of their decisions will produce effects reaching
far beyond their own lifetimes, indefinitely into future
civilization. Provisions for children or other heirs provides
some partly rational ground for these decisions. But I do not
know whether there is a rational norm for the amount
of investment to be chosen by an individual, either Crusoe
or a member of society; the question seems to have no
definite answer. Another point needing emphasis is that
an investment in technology is an investment for the infinite

future in a special sense, because new techniques do not require maintenance. Most forms of new resources do not naturally last forever; they can be maintained, or they can be used up or allowed to wear out, but this is not true of technology. However, changes in technology are so inseparably connected with changes in resources that a sharp distinction cannot be made, even though the two things are conceptually quite different. All of which is to say again that there are many limitations to the concept of economically rational behavior.

As soon as Crusoe begins to make any kind of change, he has to have a concept of capital, if he is to act rationally. What we mean by capital is productive capacity in the abstract, capacity subject to quantitative increase or decrease, or to change in form without quantitative change. I know I cannot argue this sufficiently here to make it very clear; in classes I never get it into the heads of most students, however much time I take. But again I submit as self-evident truth that the form of capital may be changed without changing the quantity, and vice versa, and that is terribly important for sound and "realistic" analysis. Obviously the main way in which we move resources from one place to another is by dis-investing and re-investing. They are not moved as they stand, but through obsolescence and replacement with a more or less different kind. The reapportionment of capital becomes very much simpler in a growing economy, because we do not actually have to move much of it: the proportions employed in different uses can be changed through differential growth of investment. There are a lot of problems in capital theory that I cannot go into here, but these problems are real and everywhere and always present, and have to be dealt with in accord with general principles—as far as possible. But there is not any completely satisfactory handling on strict principles of economic rationality alone. Yet to make any decision rationally—and we must still talk about this concept although it is realistically impossible—a Crusoe or any economizing subject would have to know the rate of return on investment in every type of resource that calls for maintenance or is subject to increase or decrease or change in form. He would have to know not only the marginal yield on investment in general, but also the yield received or to be had on investment in every separate activity conducted or considered.

I stress all this about capital and its rate of yield with an animus—or animosity, if you like—against John Maynard Keynes, later Lord Keynes, who corrupted thinking by teaching that the rate of interest is a monetary phenomenon. One main reason for stressing the Crusoe economy is to get rid of that notion: a Crusoe economy would obviously have no place for lending money or for money itself, or thinking of any such connection. A moment's reflection on the Crusoe situation should make it clear that a purely monetary theory of interest is simply nonsense. If interest is defined as payment for a loan of money then the possibility of change in its purchasing power may influence the contractual rate; but the main determinant is a thing that rational economic activity would have to take into account in every decision made, under any circumstances. To be completely rational, Crusoe would, of course, have to know practically everything. It would require virtual omniscience to make all decisions in a completely rational way, especially accurate prediction of all conditions and the consequences of his acts as far ahead as changes would make any difference in his plans. This again makes the whole rationality assumption rather fantastic if taken literally. Accordingly, when I am talking with an orthodox economist who expounds all these economic principles as gospel, I am a rip-roaring institutionalist, and when I am talking to an institutionalist who claims the principles don't make any sense at all, I defend the system, the "orthodoxy" that is treated with so much contempt by followers of Veblen and others who wear the institutionalist label.

We come now to our second main division, the economic organization, where we attempt to explain the structure and working of the market or enterprise economy. That is what economics is really about—this organization; all the business about individual behavior is preliminary and introductory, though necessary. Our practical interest, in particular, centers in the social organization of free enterprise, what it is and how it works, but this is to be understood with a view to possible improvement. I must summarize rapidly, and can only hope to be a little bit intelligible. Again I think we need to develop a picture of the kind of economy we have by beginning with highly simplified assumptions and proceeding by stages. First, we should recognize that a society could conceivably exist and be a society without any economic organization at all. It could be made up of self-sufficient units, individuals or families, each one using its own resources to satisfy its own wants and making investments out of them for the future if it wanted to. No specialization, no economic organization or cooperation, would be present. This conception is needed for contrast, and it was approximated in the manorial life of the Middle Ages.

The next stage to be considered would be an exchange economy, simpliciter—a real exchange economy based on the exchange of products in markets in which, again, the individual or family members of society would be units. But now each unit would be producing a particular product—not all the products it consumes, but some particular one. The final products would be exchanged in perfect markets. There have to be perfect markets if a definite theory is to fit the situation. At this stage we hardly need to assume any money; one of the most troublesome things in economics is the disturbing role of money and exchange, which it also greatly facilitates. We would thus have this exchange economy, the literal meaning, or a handicraft economy a suitable name. In considerable part it was a stage in the evolution of the modern economy. In the late Middle Ages and early modern times craftsmen in the towns made special products and sold them in the markets, in contrast with enterprise economy, where no individual produces a product. This is wholly untypical nowadays: products are produced in elaborate organizations producing stages of products, multiproducts, and all sorts of combinations. The exchange economy concept is a simplification, but we get a lot of things clearer if we simplify this way. In such an economy there would not be any purchase or sale of productive services, nor any incomes in the form of rent, wages, interest, or profits. These categories would not exist. Each unit would consume the income derived from the sale of its product; distribution in that sense would be something entirely different from what is treated in our economic theory. This simpler situation is important because realistic society is partly the same and partly different: old forms survive but new ones are added. That is why we need to build it up by adding successive complications until we get as near to reality as we can by theorizing.

At the next stage we deal with organized production. Products are made by complex units, plants, industries, and so forth. Instead of producing a product, an individual worker performs some detailed operation. These production units could be organized in various ways, and one of the interesting questions is why they take the form they do, in general the entrepreneurial form. Why aren't they producers' cooperatives? Why don't the laborers, owners of capital, and other renderers of services that work in a big factory agree to cooperate and determine their various productive roles and the distribution of the proceeds of the business? Why do they have to have a "boss," and accept the very unequal incomes they get? Here is where the big rumpus comes in, in modern society. Why have this entrepreneur, this despot and alleged exploiter for his own profit? Why don't they just work it out on a basis of equity? Or, for that matter, why don't the laborers hire the capital and the managers instead of being hired as they are? Of course there are reasons. We cannot go far into them here, but the general reason that this system exists is because it is the system on which the parties concerned are able to agree. If the people involved could agree on any other system, there is no law against their having any other arrangement, no impediment whatever to having production carried on, for example, in what is called a producers' cooperative if the people can make it work. The fact is, they cannot: it has been tried and failed often enough to make that clear. Being the kind of people they are, with the kind of predilections they have, they do agree on the entrepreneurial system and its functions—apart from occasional interruptions by a strike, or a bankruptcy and liquidation.

So, we have an entrepreneurial organization in which somebody or some small group that *can* agree among themselves, take charge, decide what is to be done, apportion the roles of the different operatives and different pieces of property used in the operation, and give the orders that constitute the role of "management." That figure we call the entrepreneur. This word, as you doubtless know, is French and has displaced the term "undertaker" found in the earlier English usage, which has acquired a different meaning. He is the functionary who does two things: he makes the decisions and he takes the risks—the two are inseparable. Whoever makes the responsible decisions automatically assumes the risk involved in whether those decisions turn out to be correct or more or less in error. Some confusion arises relative to the hired manager—the man who immediately makes the decisions, in relation to the notorious absentee owner. But whoever appoints the direct manager is responsible for what the latter does, he is the one who makes the *responsible* decisions in selecting his agent and giving him powers, and he is the one who takes the risk. The results of decisions cannot be predicted in advance, and this type of risk, which I have called uncertainty, is very different from that met with in a game of chance, and from the risk that can be covered by insurance based on statistics and actuarial calculations.

So we get a general picture of a society in which entrepreneurs hire the productive services, give them directions, and assure the workers or property owners an income, larger or smaller, according to their worth to the enterprise; what each adds to its total value-output. The entrepreneurs competitively hire the other productive services in the market. I say "other," though the entrepreneur's own function really is not a productive service in at all the same sense. His income, his profit, is not received as the price of any-

thing. Market competition fixes the prices he pays and those
he receives. The former, his costs of production, may add
up to more or less than the resources actually turn out to
yield, what the product will sell for. If less, the entrepreneur
makes a profit; if more, he takes a loss. If on the average
entrepreneurs bid the prices of the productive services up
too high, they suffer a loss as a group. If they do not bid
prices up high enough to balance out they break even
or make a gain as a group. They make gains on the average
and as a whole if they are pessimistic in their predictions
of results, and a loss if they are overoptimistic. Their predictions depend largely on estimates of their own capacities
to make things go. My opinion is—I can only state this conviction, not prove it, though what statistical information
there is supports it—that on the average the entrepreneur
class is optimistic, and accordingly as a group they tend
to incur loss rather than make a gain. In honesty, the
so-called profit system should be called the profit-*and-loss*
or the profit-*seeking* system, to avoid implying that there
is any such income share as profit, in the aggregate. No such
category appears in the available statistics of distribution.
Even including monopoly gain, no profit shows up. We
know that monopoly income exists; but monopolies also
make losses, though my own guess is that they are profitable
in the aggregate. To determine empirically whether all
enterprises make losses or gains in the aggregate is a hard
task; one would have to average everything over a long
period of time, and a lot of things would have to remain
equal that never do so we can never answer that question
in that way. Yet people go on ranting about the wickedness
of profit—while trying to grab it, and while the evidence
indicates that on the whole it is a minus quantity.

One of the things most needful to straighten thinking about entrepreneurship is to get the property prejudice out of the picture, since property owning has no necessary connection with the issue. The entrepreneurial relation would arise just the same if there were no such thing as property—scarce property—yielding an advantage and commanding a payment for its use. Any two workers deciding to work together with their bare hands would confront all the problems—what is to be done, what each is to do, and how to distribute the fruits of their joint activity. They must arrange cooperation, which is the function performed by entrepreneurs and competitive markets. The word is misleading, as I have said before; competition in the primary sense of rivalry is antithetical to the economic motive, and we should have something quite different in mind when we speak of the competitive system; it is a system of cooperation. We have to try to get the public to understand this if we are going to stop the foolish war of words. People who have to work together might conceivably negotiate everything out in advance or as they go along, making all decisions jointly by agreement *ad hoc*. But one can hardly imagine real human beings doing it. Manifestly it is vastly simpler for one of them to take charge and agree to give the others a predetermined amount of the product, with the organizer taking the gains, if any, or the loss if the activity does not make enough to pay what he has agreed to pay his partners. For this he must have resources of his own, though *as entrepreneur* he does not own anything. Actually, the persons acting as entrepreneurs are usually both workers and property owners as well; some part of their income is really of wages and a part is yield of property, and this must be allowed for to arrive at the pure profit.

This brings us to something that should be said about forms of property income. The ordinary direct way for the entrepreneur to get the use of property is by lease, paying a rent. Then interest, which the classical economists (and Marx) did not distinguish from profit, must be explained. It has gotten all involved along with the capital concept and monetary relations in a way that has led, I think, to the worst confusion in economic thinking. To me it is self-evident that, if both parties know what they are doing and there is a free market, it does not make any difference whether the prospective user of a piece of property rents it from the owner or borrows the money and buys it—in the one case paying rent, and in the other interest. They are equivalent alternatives in so far as the parties involved foresee the consequences and act intelligently. In many situations the two procedures are indeed a matter of practical indifference: people rent farms, or they borrow the money and buy them and pay interest rather than rent. Similarly, one buys a house, he pays interest—or loses interest that he could have got, which is the same thing—or, alternatively, he may rent the house. Only special considerations involving speculative uncertainties make a difference, causing one of these alternatives to be chosen by agreement rather than the other. If the farm owner leases the land to the farm operator and the land changes in value, the farm owner gets the gain or suffers the loss. If he sells the land to the operator, it is the latter, now owner (but for him it is no net asset) who gets any gain or suffers loss. It comes down to a difference of opinion, as Pudd'nhead Wilson said about hoss-races. Further, the mere fact that values may change, will still make no material difference if they are equally optimistic or pessimistic about the future; the changes will appear on both the demand and supply offers fixing the sale price on which agreement will be reached, compared with the equivalent rental, for a contract over any period.

It is not quite the same thing when one wants the use of, say, an automobile owned by another; for, what will happen to the car, affecting its value, may be more dependent on the user's sense of responsibility, and that may be more affected by the difference in ownership. The difference is limited, however. The treatment of a farm also will naturally be more or less different in the two cases—which is the reason tenancy is considered bad for society. A renting farmer is inclined to "mine out" the soil, while an owner-operator will have reason to maintain it or build it up—and similarly for the buildings and other improvements. Details would take us into history, and differences between countries and regions. Tenancy has worked out differently in England than it has in the American Middle West—or South—because of customary terms of leasing and the presence or absence of laws or effective customs safeguarding long-run social interests.

What is in point just here is the *rate* of interest, per cent per annum, or some specified interval. If we assume adequate foreknowledge for both parties, and economically rational behavior, the *amount* of the interest to be paid annually will as shown be identical with an annual rental acceptable to both: either sum will be the imputed yield to be expected from the property. The *rate* of interest is then a matter of the capital value of the property in question—which effective competition will make identical over the economy for all property of equal yield, after provision for perpetuity and with allowance for risk and various costs. The difficulty that has caused confusion here is that for property already existing and under stable conditions, the value is derived by capitalizing the expected yield at a going rate, as a given; the value is the dependent variable, the unknown in a fairly simple equation. For the factors determining the going rate, we must look to the field where new investments are being made. For simplicity we may think of a progressive economy, one in which total investment is growing substantially; the reasoning is easily modified to fit a stationary or a retrogressive situation, with net disinvestment. The person considering any investment must estimate the prospective yield of the new "productive agents"—including every kind of source of income—and relate this to their cost-of-production to obtain the expected rate of yield. With effective competition, the value will simply be the cost. (Many details must be ignored here, particularly mathematical complications due to diverse conditions.) There always is a more or less definite current rate for borrowing or lending, and a prospective investor can simplify his thinking by comparing this with the estimated prospect of any new investment, or different opportunities, under consideration; and according as the one or the other is better, a particular "real" investment will or will not be made.

The next task is to consider what will happen to the going rate as further new investment is made, which must be assumed to occur all over the economy and in all kinds of opportunities, at a uniform net rate, under ideal conditions. Here I strongly take issue with the common assumption that growth of investment will lower the quality of opportunities open and hence the rate of yield—the traditional dogma of diminishing returns from investment. In any case, the decline would be quite slow, since new investment is added to all that has been made in the past, and over any moderate period of foresight will be small in comparison with the latter. Moreover, and more important, even the assumption of a gradual decline rests on palpably fallacious reasoning. It would be sound only under *ceteris-paribus* conditions that are grossly unrealistic. The fallacy is neglecting large fields of investment that *raise* the demand (the whole curve) in the field actually considered—the creation of "capital goods" narrowly defined. In a "dynamic" economy a vast amount of investment goes into opening up new fields, through introducing new products or new technology in older lines, and exploring natural resources. At bottom is the fallacious assumption that capital is added to a given supply of other factors, that are fixed in supply, and so is used in less and less favorable proportions to these—in conventional thinking, to "labor" and "natural agents." But the least reflection must show that much investment is made both in exploring and developing new so-called natural agents and also in increasing the supply of labor, both numbers and quality. And besides, as just indicated, "technology," broadly defined, with scientific research as its basis, is in essential respects a productive factor, a form of capital. It has special features, as does any class, but it is increased at a cost, and expected to yield a return on its cost, in competition with other investment opportunities.

Two facts are essential: First, that investment in these three neglected fields raises the demand-curve for capital-goods as traditionally conceived; and secondly, that all three are highly explorative and the result to be expected from any venture highly unpredictable. On balance, the direction or "sign" of any effect on the yield rate, due to new investment as a whole, is also unpredictable; it may either raise or lower the rate, so far as we know; it is as likely to work in

one direction as in the other. And in any case it is only a
tendency over a limited time. This view is in accord with
history. Periods in which technological advance and growth
of the other two factors have predominated and raised the
going rate-of-interest have alternated with periods in which
the opposite has been the case (as far as the going rate
itself is known, which it is not with any accuracy). Thus
neither in theory nor in historical fact is there any tendency
to lower the rate, or any meaningful tendency towards
a stationary equilibrium rate—as argued by Marshall and
others. And still less can one defend a natural equilibrium at
a zero level (Schumpeter, Keynes, et al.). The rate could
quite well go below zero, under conditions that one can
imagine, though not realistically foresee. (I cannot here
go into the effects of monetary changes on predictability
and on the rate for contractual borrowing for various inter-
vals in the money market; that is an important problem, but
in my opinion is not very amenable to economic analysis,
and has been over-exploited of late, under the influence of
the Great Depression and of "Keynesism.")

I now turn very briefly to a conspicuous feature of the
modern economic organization—the growth of "corporate"
enterprise as the typical form of entrepreneurship. For two
main reasons, this development creates highly important
practical problems, calling for social action. The first is that
the large size of business units reduces their number in any
market, and may facilitate monopoly, or at least give rise
to a form of imperfect competition known as oligopoly (with
oligopsony as a theoretical counterpart). The former is a
situation in which a few units, especially large units, turn
out somewhat differentiated products or operate in somewhat

distinct markets, in one sense or another. One important result is lavish and more or less wasteful advertising, in an effort to exaggerate the favorable difference between a product and competing physical goods or services, by using brand-names. The second reason is the power of management in large aggregations of property and labor—increasingly separated from ownership, and distorting if not corrupting the theoretical role of the entrepreneur. Thus arise the twofold problem of a power relation of corporate officials over the titular owners of the property employed and the working force. The latter is exaggerated by the spokesmen of labor, who demand that it be offset by the countervailing power of vast labor unions, which are even more undemocratic in their control than the corporation. Then there is the power of the corporate unit over consumers, in so far as success attends the inevitable effort to establish monopoly.

It is impossible here to take up in detail any of these problem situations. The main observation in point is that the importance of the second and third evils—corporate monopoly and arbitrary power over labor—while sometimes real, are not universal, and their extent and importance are enormously exaggerated in popular thinking, rooted in an inherent prejudice against business, and urged on by labor propaganda. The popular view seems to be that monopoly is a fine thing, if operated by and for any special interest except business, notably labor and the farmer. The social cost of these other monopolies or equivalent restrictionists is enormously greater than that of business monopoly, particularly because the latter has long been recognized (and exaggerated) and strenuous efforts have been made at legal prevention or curbing, while the former are strongly encouraged by public action.

The large size and composite nature of the corporate enterprises are unimportant for general theory, since the competitive or monopolistic analysis still applies—as long, that
is, as the unit is controlled by the economic motive of profit-
seeking, not by internal struggles for power or for gain by
any component interest at the expense of others, or by
political activities. The nature of entrepreneurship and profit
is still the same, as long as it is an open game; anyone who
thinks he can make resources yield more than the current
market rate may become an entrepreneur, and if his judgment of the situation and of his capacities is justified by
events, he will make a profit; otherwise, he will incur a loss
or may break even. The tendency of market competition is
to set the remuneration paid to labor and property at what
they can be made to yield—deviating upward or downward
in particular cases—with a similar compensation for the
entrepreneur's own contribution of property or personal
services. In a fair sample of cases, deviations should cancel
out, equalizing gain and loss, unless there is a systematic
bias in entrepreneurial judgments. It seems to me fairly
certain that there is such a bias—that, as already suggested,
entrepreneurs in general are optimistic in estimating their
prospects or their capacities or both. In consequence they
receive on the average less than the going rate for their
substantive contribution, and so incur a loss, besides getting
no payment for the distinctive, socially indispensable function of entrepreneurship. The loss may come out of their
own labor or property earnings, or be passed on to creditors,
who share in the entrepreneur function in so far as they
subject themselves to this risk. Society seems to get this most
vital of all economic functions performed at no cost, or
less than none. Entrepreneurs are paid for their efforts and

losses—like outright gamblers as a class—by the excitement of the game, and by pride in bossing rather than being bossed. Objectors to the free-enterprise order should at least compare it with the possible alternatives, which would be one or another form of socialism, probably an authoritarian dictatorship.

It remains to note that there is a special kind of profit associated with lending at interest. One who borrows money for the usual business purpose of creating productive assets for his own operations expects to make a gain both on the loan itself, in comparison with buying or leasing existing property, and then on operating the acquired assets, in comparison with selling or leasing them to someone else. For complex but fairly obvious reasons, corporate enterprises usually secure the use of property from outsiders more largely through borrowing, on bonds or other credit instruments than through leasing. Particular features of the free enterprise organization, like the system as a whole, prevail in so far as they are more satisfactory than alternative modes of cooperation to all the parties concerned.

Chapter IV ~ THE ECONOMIC ORDER: GENERAL PROBLEMS

In the preceding lecture I suggested as a difficulty in factual description and analysis of social phenomena that it seems to be nearly impossible to adopt a really objective attitude, to see them as they are, and not to adopt an attitude of either apology or negative criticism. I recently ran onto a quotation I had read long ago, a statement by Ruskin in which he called Adam Smith a half-bred and half-witted Scotsman who, in founding the dismal science of political economy, uttered the deliberate blasphemy that men should hate God and despise His commandments and covet their neighbors' goods. This is a somewhat florid statement of what the world at large seems to think about us political economists.

I shall start this lecture by noting that there are two sets of problems for policy or action: problems arising because the system does not work in accordance with the theoretical description, and problems arising because it does. I also remarked that it was the one main error in public thinking generally to overstress the first set, to think that everything that is wrong or not ideal (according to somebody's ideal) is that way because the system does not work according to the theory and that if only the perfect competition described by the pure theory were real, then everything would be lovely, but the competition is a myth and business is everywhere monopolistic. You hear talk all the time that neglects the palpable fact that the system could not possibly operate in the real world if monopoly were at all general or in strict accord with the theory; general principles such as these must be abstract to be analytically correct and useful. Pure theory has to be built in this field, and anywhere else for that matter, in terms of relations that very incompletely describe the facts of nature. However, to my mind, the complaint does point to a somewhat paradoxical fact. On the one hand, economic theory describes what superficially sounds much like an ideal social order, the social order of "perfect cooperation," based on mutual advantage. This theoretical system achieves maximum possible efficiency from the use of available resources, with everybody completely free to choose, among the alternatives open, in consumption and in production, and it apportions to each participant a share in the joint product precisely in accord with what he contributes to it.

Now these results are true for the ideal theoretical working of a free-enterprise economy, implying perfect atomistic exchange or what is called perfect competition. If all the given conditions were really in complete accord with the idealizing assumptions, the situation would seem to be perfectly ideal. But the reality is not an ideal situation, and few think it is; nor would it be even if the world were such that practice could follow theory exactly, which cannot possibly be the case. The present task is to show some of the reasons why—with the facts of nature, man, and society what they are—the framework of free enterprise does not at all imply an ideal social order.

Postponing temporarily the question of ideals, I shall take up first what I have gotten into the habit of calling the mechanical problems, the shortcomings of the system as an individualistic economic organization. Following this, I shall take up other problems which are not mechanistic or organizational, if they are really economic problems at all. Everywhere we confront distinctions that are necessary but vague and difficult to state with any degree of clarity. There are again two main sets of these mechanical problems which arise because the system does not work in accord with the theoretical exposition: problems of monopoly and monopoloid situations, and those of cyclical oscillations. Both are rather hackneyed subjects, and I do not want to spend too much time on them; I shall run briefly over a few observations, and go on to more social-philosophical issues which seem to me much more interesting and more neglected.

It is particularly in connection with monopoly that the public has grossly exaggerated ideas. There is nothing like as much monopoly, especially business monopoly, as the public thinks there is. A good deal of what there is is beneficial, and a good deal of it is contrived in the social interest, as when the law grants patents and copyrights and the like. All profit is in principle monopoly profit, due to friction temporarily limiting mobility of resources. The expectation of such profits, arising out of temporary and partial monopoly, functions as patents are intended to, as the incentive or lure to induce people to try to make useful innovations. On the whole, profit, including so-called monopoly profit, is not an evil except where it is too much or is maintained too long—and there is no definite standard for saying when it is too high or lasts too long. Normal profit is probably at least fully offset by losses, again including monopoly gains; even the most extreme monopoly may lose money, and all are limited by the competition of substitutes.

There are, what are called "natural monopolies," situations

in which conditions prevent effective competition, such as street railways and municipal telephone systems. Here some action must be taken, and the obvious solution is for the society to take over the enterprise and operate it through some political agency. But this obvious solution is not necessarily the right or best one since we have the alternative of legally controlled prices, and must consider the weaknesses of politics in managing business. Conclusions here depend very largely on which organization, the economic or the political system, one thinks more trustworthy.

The worst monopolies are by no means those in business. Labor unions and restrictionist farm organizations supported by public opinion and political action are far more likely to raise prices by restricting production. These are much more costly to society and are unjustifiable on any grounds, though the organizations have other quite legitimate functions. This again reflects the general prejudice against business. I still think Adam Smith is largely right: if the government would keep its hands clean of encouraging monopolies, much of the problem would very largely take care of itself. Not all, of course, but certainly the labor and farm monopolies would be harmless, and corporate monopolies, where at all serious, could be fairly well handled through sensible corporation laws, granting reasonably limited powers, accompanied by positive action to keep open the channels of entry into industries and occupations.

The importance of the prejudice against business can hardly be overstressed. The major requirement for intelligent economic policy is to get people to take an objective attitude rather than to think that monopoly in particular, and even violence up to arson and mayhem if not murder is right or wrong depending on who does it. I noted before that the same conduct is considered terribly wicked if it is done by business and quite virtuous and deserving of approval and support if it is done by or for labor or the farmer. Mentioning the farmer makes me think of another general, primitive prejudice. That is the physiocratic one, to the effect that only agriculture really produces anything, that other people only pass goods along and take a toll on the traffic. You can see that in every newspaper every day; there is some kick about the middleman, especially about the farmer not getting what he produces because so much is skimmed off along the way to the consumer by these collectors of toll. I am not saying that middleman functions are never developed to excess, leading to waste or that middlemen never reap large gains, legitimately or otherwise, as in other lines, respecting both bad allocation of resources and excessive gains (though the latter are cancelled by losses in the group as a whole). In any case the prejudice is there, and the point is that people who make these criticisms do not try to weigh possible alternatives, or even look at the high incidence of loss and bankruptcy in this field. This is of a piece with the dogmas that his employer owes every worker some standard of living irrespective of his value to the enterprise, or that consumers of farm products have the same obligation to every farmer. The mixing of moral sentiment or prejudice into judgments of fact and causality works to the utter confusion of thought, as it has done all through history. Of course the apologetic can go the other way and be as corrupting.

I shall not have time to go back into classical political economy, to discuss the nonsense talked by the great writers such as Smith and Ricardo, in which economic analysis was in part vitiated by this moralizing, condemning, or approving attitude in place of trying to analyze objectively. With them it worked both ways, but came to a main focus, of course, in the labor theory of value. This again is in every newspaper every day, and literature (*belles lettres*) is full of it. Survival from savagery of an animistic and anthropomorphic world view in modern human nature causes the whole product of society to be treated as, and be called, the productivity of labor. Marx copied this theory and in general the worst features of his system from Ricardo—and differed by drawing the logical conclusions; and the same is true of Henry George with the palpable but popular fallacy of the "single tax." But this also harks back to the Physiocrats who were largely followed by Smith also, and J. S. Mill (in spite of some criticisms Smith made of the Agricultural System). Men have yet to learn not to confuse causality with moral desert—usually in a sentimental version—to the corruption of both concepts.

The second of the two mechanical problems I have mentioned is the tendency of production in particular industries or branches and especially in the economy as a whole to move in oscillatory expansions and declines, the over-all fluctuations which we call the business cycle. One of the early propagandists for the Russian system, a man called Ilyin, used this oscillation very effectively to satirize the capitalist system. His example was hat manufacture: when the hat industry is profitable, Knox, Lox, and Box, and all the rest go into it until the world is flooded with hats; then everyone goes out of that industry and nobody has any hats. Well there is some of that tendency in reality. To go into that would be to develop the theory of cycles, and this is not my function or intention this evening. I would repeat that not all the stupidity, the inane criticism of the economic order, is confined to the public. No small part of it may be explained as a reaction of common sense against essentially stupid or needlessly unrealistic things that economists have said about the economic order and the tendency toward equilibrium. An economy that settles down quickly and operates smoothly, that runs along in a position at or near the theoretical equilibrium is, of course, rather fanciful, and is not predicted by sound theory. Nearly all the automatic adjustments, the responses, are subject to greater or less lag, resulting naturally in more or less extreme oscillations such as occur in any automatic regulatory system—as the governor of an engine, the thermostat on a furnace, or the like. The period and the amplitude of these oscillations is a question for the theory of the appropriate branch of inquiry. In the case of the business cycle, particularly in industry, the period and amplitude are apparently impossible to explain in detail, though the general causality of the "swings" is hardly mysterious. Details are to be found out empirically, and predictions made from what they have been.

When I was just a lad I was interested in the corn-hog cycle, which was at that time about four years. The cattle cycle was about fourteen years. In many cases there is an exaggerating effect: when it is profitable to feed hogs, people not only feed more hogs but to do so they withdraw hogs from the market for breeding purposes and tend to accentuate the current high price. Until after the breeding period, a year and a half or so, there is a trooping into the hog business. Overdevelopment follows, and it does not immediately swing the other way, or the cycle would not be four years. This phenomenon is not very hard to explain. In the case of apple trees, the time it takes a tree to come into fruit-bearing age is about ten years, and I believe the cycle has been about twenty or thirty years. Again, when apples are profitable people will probably both raise apples from existing orchards, and set out more trees. (They might neglect the former activity in favor of the latter, if resources are not available from outside the industry and so increase the shortage, as in the case of hogs.) When apples from all those trees that are planted in the period of shortage begin to be put on the market, there is a disaster.

The same general sort of thing happens in the economy as a whole in the investment market. Why it happens all over the place with some degree of simultaneity is undoubtedly because of the phenomenon of money. I know this is disputed, but I think the argument is largely a dispute over words. I am not an expert on the business cycle, but I insist that it is fundamentally a phenomenon of oscillation in the purchasing power of money, due to changes in the quantity of money or of money substitutes, or in its velocity of circulation, or both. Whenever prices are tending to rise or people think they are going to rise, the tendency is to try to turn money into goods by purchase and increased production, to get the benefit of the high prices. It is more profitable to hold real assets than to hold money. That makes business prosperous, primarily in durable goods industries. The prices of goods go up, which continues to encourage investment and overproduction, until the thing comes to a head, collapses, and begins to go the other way. If people are pessimistic, of course, the reverse happens. When they expect general prices to fall, they want to convert goods into money, especially to stop purchasing or creating new durable goods. The investment market slumps, and this is where the major unemployment occurs. I do not think that it is very hard to explain the expansion and contraction of the investment market, or the alternating boom with depression and idle resources.

The ultimate difficulty with the free economy is that everybody needs to know what everybody else is going to do before he can decide intelligently what he will do. And of course that is impossible—literally and strictly impossible. If people predict each other's actions and act on the predictions, they will falsify those predictions. The only way to get accurate anticipation of other people's action is by pre-concerting the program; but that is directly contrary to individualistic principles and would immediately involve monopoly and collusion. Planning must be integral, and that requires compulsory political action. The problem is to find the best compromise between freedom and order—how much to leave to individual free choice and voluntary agreement versus what limits to set by enforced general rules.

Much more could be said about cycle theory. Commercial banking is a device that might have been invented by the devil for multiplying all these bad effects, but we still have it in spite of the fact that some eminent economists have advocated 100 per cent bank reserves. Irving Fisher, I believe, started this proposal some time before the First World War, if not longer ago. However if we got rid of fractional reserve banking, it would not be any guarantee against general expansion and contraction of the money circulation. Nevertheless, Fisher's proposal certainly is in the right direction. This finally leads into the other side of the whole picture: the political order, in relation to which the economic order exists and through which it has to be controlled. The evils of the economic order must be dealt with, if at all, by the government—that organization or agency by which a society acts as a unit, or simply by which a society acts. A monetary system in particular will not function automatically or be stable without control. The natural tendency for money to rise and fall in value more or less cyclically is not limited in amplitude and period by fundamental conditions such as exist in other speculative markets. In any such speculative markets prices tend alternately to rise until they are well above the equilibrium level, and then they fall until they are more or less below it. But in the case of raising and marketing hogs or wheat, fluctuations are kept within bounds by men's knowledge of real demand and real supply. People in the market try to operate on the basis of expectations founded on the reality, and they can estimate the equilibrium position; hence, when the situation gets clearly away from the equilibrium very far in either direction, they act in a way to reverse the trend. The speculators' interest is to operate in such a way so as to push the market back toward equilibrium. With general prices, the knowledge of normality is too vague and uncertain to prevent swings—booms and depressions that are too serious for passive toleration.

It is now generally admitted that the money system has to be controlled. The controversy that persists among the economists is over the question whether it can be controlled according to rules enacted in law, or whether it requires a lot of discretionary power on the part of the administrators. The issue is partly what rules to lay down but is largely one of degree, as to how definite the rules can be. I lean rather strongly toward the side of administrative discretion and judgment, being skeptical about how far rules can be made in advance or especially how far they would be made wisely by the agencies that would in fact make them. If we do not trust administrative authority acting in the situation of the moment—and I admit all the dangers of that—we have to

trust legislative authority to foresee conditions in advance
and enact suitable rules, which must be precise as to amount
and timing of action; and then an administrative authority
must be trusted to interpret and apply them. It seems to me
we are between the devil and the sea. Where are we going
to draw the line, and where can we get authorities to make
constitutional and public law in line with what experts
think?

Economic theory assumes perfect markets which either
approximate ideal competition or show some particular
degree of monopoly. (General monopolies palpably are impossible; the system would blow up completely.) In theoretical analysis we usually think of the system as ideally
competitive, meaning simply the minimum of monopoly.
Any doctor or painter, for example, has a monopoly of his
particular service or product. But the ideally competitive
system is impossible; in the limit, the ideal of freedom
becomes self-contradictory. There cannot be a perfect market
subject to change, unless it is an infinitely gradual change. If
equilibrium existed at some moment, any change in conditions would upset it, and then the tendency would be to
oscillate; and theoretically the system would oscillate forever,
in the absence of friction. With friction present, oscillation
once started would go on indefinitely but at an ever de-
creasing amplitude, as long as conditions remained un-
changed—assuming friction on the analogy of viscosity. Pour
a perfect fluid into one end of a long trough and it will
oscillate back and forth forever at a constant amplitude. With
molasses the flow would continue in one direction, while
with sand the position will soon be stationary but not at a
level position. Yet economists have talked about frictionless
conditions; we all do, and I think we have to, but we

should be clear about the abstraction and lack of realism. One thing I have thought should be done in economic theory is to investigate the analogies implied by the use of terms like inertia, momentum, and friction. I know of only one attempt to do that at all seriously, and it did not get very far. The idea of a continuing perfect equilibrium in an economy with any degree of freedom is highly unrealistic. We usually talk about the perfectly competitive adjustment or equilibrium at two levels. The adjustment can be approximately realized in the market for any one product or a productive service, but in an entrepreneurial system, the entrepreneurs cannot possibly be in anything like effective competition among themselves, because it is their business to deal with uncertainties, both with the uncertainties produced by conditions beyond their control and with others which it is their function to produce, by initiating departures looking toward improvement or progress.

Many of the same or similar problems exist on the consumption side of the economic order, as contrasted with the business side I have been talking about. A society made up of economic men, even as consumers, would be a fantastic monstrosity and a physical impossibility. Nor have I mentioned the worst limitations. The more serious ones arrive in a more or less border line field between economics and other aspects of social relations, social psychology and so forth. One of the most neglected is the game aspect, the competitive sport aspect, of economic life itself, along with other forms of play, and the gambling appeal. This play aspect is in my opinion, or conjecture, as large and important from the standpoint of values and social policy as it is from the standpoint of its role in satisfying people's economic wants. I must say that as I have turned these questions over and over in my mind through the years, I have come to take less seriously the whole idea of maximum satisfaction as depicted by economic theory, the maximum satisfaction of given wants, as an algebraic function, by a rational and correct allocation of consumers' expenditure and use of productive resources. I take more seriously the play aspect and the fact of freedom as itself a value, a value in both senses of the word. Not only do people want freedom as such, but also, in so far as men can have any ethical ideals at all, they must think people ought to be free, within limits, whether they want to be or not. In fact, our laws and acts in society, in preventing slavery and limiting the power to contract out future freedom, recognize this position to a considerable extent and impose compulsory freedom. People are not allowed to sell themselves into servitude or to make contracts for very far in the future, binding themselves personally, which would of course mean servitude enforced by law. The general rule is that personal service contracts are not legally enforceable. They are made, to some extent, and enforced by other means. The most familiar example is the contracts of stars in baseball, which are bought and sold. If people are free, the more completely their needs are met, the less important become the desires for particular goods and services, in comparison with interesting activities. I think it is as important to make activity interesting as it is to make it efficient. This of course is not true until production reaches a level that supports a decent physical standard of living. Efficiency is always important, but as people move higher up the scale, it becomes less so.

I want to go into this particularly, the matter of efficiency, in my next lecture, in connection with ethics; there are several things about it that are very interesting. One point

is that there is no place for the play interest, particularly
that of competitive sport, in our traditional religious ethics,
while on the other hand there is no place for charity in a
game. When charity comes in the game goes out; people
have to play to win and, in that sense, to follow a selfish
interest. There are lots of problems here that are more or
less on the border line between the social organization
problems and the ethical problem, and many of them are to
my mind unanswerable. I have never been able to formulate
the definition of an economic want that has any concrete
meaning, and must protest against the idea that economics
deals merely with subsistence, the animal needs, or the
cruder comfort wants, or anything of that sort. The notion
of economizing applies to, and the economic organization
deals with, all activities which rationally use given means
to achieve given ends. But what is the degree of realism of
the conception of conduct in terms of the use of given means
to achieve the given ends? This rather stumps me; ends are
means, and vice-versa, and the relation is never sharp or
clear.

Even more am I puzzled as to what to say about the
rationality or moral quality of the activities of competitive
sport itself; it is certainly not rational in the sense of using
means efficiently to achieve a foreseen end. The end sought
is to win, which cancels out, since for every victory there
is a defeat. The instrumental motivation is attenuated, since
unpredictability is an essential part of the interest, and
moreover is inverted. The players do, indeed, strive to
achieve a specific end, to score in some way—to push a ball
over a line or knock one out of reach, or whatever is done
to "take a trick" from an opponent. But they do this in
accord with arbitrary and highly artificial rules. Victory

over an opponent, the conscious goal, is an end deliberately
set up, under conditions, to make the activity interesting.
The rational objective is a good game, for loser as well as
winner; that means at least an interesting game, and a
reasonably fair game. All this so far revolutionizes the
instrumental view of the organization, especially the ethics
of the situation. The problem becomes infinitely more
complex in economic and political reality, where the game
interest is combined with objective ends, from subsistence
needs to an infinite variety of esthetic or conventional wants,
all to be met efficiently and in accord with moral norms while
over all spreading the ethical ideal of progress.

Another puzzle is the correct treatment of technology.
What the plain man thinks of as economy is largely the
use of more efficient techniques, as well as selection of the
more important wants. For static or very short-run analysis,
the theorist treats the available technology as a given; producers are assumed to know and adopt the best processes.
There is no economic problem, apportioning means to
secure a maximum, but only an all-or-none choice among
methods. In the dynamic or long-run view, however, technology is not given, but is obviously a field of investment,
though a peculiar one. Action cannot be highly rational,
since it involves research and invention, which are highly
exploratory, as in fact all problem-solving activity is, in
the nature of the case. Our modern minds are conditioned
to thinking of thinking itself as instrumentally rational, and
in the limit that reduces to mechanistic process. In so far as
one does not know the end sought, which is the answer to
some question, conduct is not rational; and if it is known
in advance it is no problem.

Now to say a little more about the unrealism of pure

economic theory, especially the impossibility of separating economics from politics. The whole problem of social action centers in the relation between the economic order and the political order, as I have said. Any public choice, any policy decision, is properly one of comparing predictively the nature and working of these two orders in terms of values, themselves critically appraised. All the sciences of man and society are involved if one presses the question further and further back—particularly history, and possibly even more especially, ethics. We cannot make any policy decision intelligently without knowing what it is desirable to do and to attempt to do in the way of using the political order to change the economic order, to regulate it or direct it into a more desirable channel of action or whatever the problem is. In general, people tend either simply to defend the economic order as ideal, the be-all and the end-all—to say "let it alone" (*laisser faire*)—or appeal to law and government to remedy anything they think is wrong, without asking critically whether it is remediable or not, or whether politics will do it better. They rarely reflect critically about the relations between the two. Actually, the issue is never economics *or* politics; it is always a question of the best combination— not only of the best proportion, but also of the best way to integrate the tendencies of the free market system with political action.

The two orders present great similarities and important differences. The free enterprise economy is a competitive organization of economic life, and political democracy is a competitive organization of political life—in contrast with monopolistic politics, which means dictatorship. In so far as society is committed to freedom as a basic ideal, there must be a presumption in favor of the economic order because it is free in a sense and to a degree that a political order is not and cannot be. That means minimizing the role of government, carrying freedom as far as it can go, so long as it does not conflict too much with some other social value that is deemed more important, or at some point becomes so. The theoretically ideal market is ideally free; nobody has any arbitrary power over anybody else, because everybody has equal alternatives among which to choose, competitors with whom he can trade. And the real market is by no means as different in this respect from the theoretically ideal market as the critics allege. As I have said over and over, monopoly and restrictionism, though they bulk large in a quantitative sense, are comparatively unimportant in our society as a whole compared with a lot of other evils, and when present are largely due to "stupid"—obviously self-defeating or injurious—social policies. In a competitive market the participants are free in the true sense, free from arbitrary interference by the power of others. But freedom alone does not solve the social problems. There are other values that must be considered.

What troubles analysis and understanding here is that freedom has become a word to conjure with, and that is a historical anomaly. A few generations ago the opposite was the case; conformity and obedience were the moral norms of social life. Freedom has become so far identified with value in general and so useful for political propaganda that the word is defined in such a way as to beg any question for either side. It may sound dogmatic to state what is the correct definition of freedom, but I must undertake to do that, though I don't think it can be done finally or accurately. One question is the relation between freedom as a fact and as a value. Certainly we are not concerned with metaphysical freedom. Metaphysically, one choice is just as free as any other; it is only a question of the reality of choice itself, which is assumed in saying (choosing to say) anything about it or about anything. The practical issue is the alternatives open, the conditions under which one chooses. Freedom is the opposite of coercion, not of determinism. Up to a point the Spencerian definition, or the one that has been associated with Spencer, is the correct one: people should be free as long as they do not interfere with the equal freedom of other people. A free society recognizes the general right of people to exercise the freedom that is covered by the definition. But not without further sweeping limitations. While freedom is not to be confused with power, it means freedom to use power possessed, and is empty in content without control over means, hence power in some form. That is necessary to make freedom effective. Yet social freedom cannot mean the unlimited right of people possessing great economic power to use it at will, even in free exchange relations, and, in particular, to use it to get more power indefinitely. Freedom, particularly economic freedom, has to be restricted by rules, made and enforced as law by social agencies acting on behalf of the general interest. Freedom in the market organization of economic cooperation is freedom to make offers to other people and to choose the most favorable offer made by others, and that is the only freedom that is socially possible. The alternative is collusion, which limits the freedom of others and must be excluded; its name is monopoly. People do not have to exchange on the terms set by the market; they can "exchange," or make reciprocal transfers of goods or services, on any terms on which they can agree: analytically, that mixes exchange with giving and receiving gifts, which is freely allowed.

Freedom of exchange works out into the somewhat

paradoxical situation that the chief freedom you can have is a freedom to choose your boss. An illustration is the relation between a patient and a doctor. When you have chosen your doctor, you put yourself into his hands, obey his orders, and give him unlimited power, actually of life and death. All the freedom you have is that of choosing your doctor in the first place and changing him at will. It may not be a very effective freedom in the case of the doctor, as it may not be in the case of an impecunious employee of a large business enterprise. But the economy has the supreme merit that it enables any number of people to cooperate for their mutual advantage in increasing the efficiency of their individualistic activities—that is, the use of their means to achieve their ends—without agreeing, or with a minimum of agreement, on preferences in consumption and in production. It is the only possible way in which people can cooperate, and have this twofold freedom. Goods are produced and are consumed without getting a general consensus and agreement on the whole system—what is to be produced, how and by whom, and who is to get what part of the joint product.

Man is a disagreeing animal, and the hope of getting such agreement freely is practically nonexistent. The alternative to the market economy is a nonfree system operating under a dictatorship, either an individual or a group held together by a common interest in keeping power and enlarging it. The most democratic government is indefinitely less free. In so far as the economy works according to theory, it is a system of free relations. It is free largely because it is impersonal; individuals do not have to ask and answer questions of each other at all. Ideally the system could be worked out through coin-in-the-slot machines, without personal contact. Government is indefinitely less free because men must agree on the laws but do not agree at all completely through free discussion. One thinks of the historical case of Charles and Francis, who agreed perfectly, both wanting the same thing—which only one could have. That sort of agreement is typical, as is the disagreement on the terms on which they will work together, the role of each, and how to divide up the fruits of any joint effort. At most government is a matter of the dictation of a majority over minorities in whatever political unit we are considering. But even to have a real majority decision on very many particular issues is quite impossible. There is much moonshine in the talk about democracy, and it contrasts strikingly with the slurs that people perpetually cast on politics. There is as much paradox here as there is in the popular notions about the economy. An example is the romantic nonsense in the pretense of government by laws and not by men. Government is of men and by men, more or less in accord with law, and the laws are made by men and for men and again more or less in accord with constitutional law, or with some expression of the popular will, more or less definite and harmonious. Any group acts through individual agents, and the individual agents inevitably have a good deal of arbitrary power. The illustration of a doctor and patient has been mentioned; or one may consider a symphony orchestra. Everything is programmed long in advance to the last detail —to the twentieth of a second or whatever it is—by the composer, and the musicians rehearse and drill, and yet they cannot produce a decent performance without a conductor as boss. In situations where there are looser conditions and requirements, an organization without effective leadership is simply no organization.

Now a word about the major weakness in principle of the ideal of social freedom as such. Freedom pertains to given individuals; the individual must be there before he can be free. A free society means, or would mean, that all social groupings would be strictly voluntary in the sense that everyone would be free to join or to leave any group at will, and he would have to be able to do so without loss. Of course, this is fantastically impossible. In particular the state cannot be a voluntary group. It is a wishfully utopian misconception to say that it is; in reality it is enormously far from being a voluntary association. The state is rather the organization in which, next to the family, the individual has practically no choice as to whether he will belong in the first place and not much more as to whether he will remain a member when he finds himself one. It is an organization in which you are a member by compulsion. This used to apply to the church; it doesn't, nearly so much, any more, but it does apply more or less to some other organizations like, especially, trade unions. They are theoretically voluntary, but actually they are commonly not voluntary at all. Membership and conformity to the orders of their bosses are often a condition of earning a livelihood.

Here I want to insert rather in parentheses that the major real problem of defining freedom to my mind is the matter of distinguishing between being free and feeling free. People can be made to feel free, to think they are doing what they do from the freest possible choice when they are actually being manipulated entirely by somebody else, against their own interests or judgment. This is done by employing psychology —consciously or instinctively—"making them like it," to use the vulgar phrase. In economics, taking the individual as given means, of course, assuming that he has given economic attributes, wants and resources or productive capacities. In general taking the free individual as given is obviously nonsense; both the wants and the capacities of the adult are largely the product of social processes, of one's culture. With respect to children, freedom has no content. What Jefferson thought he meant by men being born equal or endowed with a natural right to freedom is a puzzle to me. We are not born free, but helpless; the idea simply has no meaning; the only meaning of equality at birth is that all are equal to zero. As to freedom, the same is true to a corresponding degree for all the dependents, all the helpless members of society, even for the temporarily incapacitated. As noted before, freedom presupposes a will—some desires— and has no content apart from control of some means of action. Otherwise, one may make choices mentally, but cannot execute them, however free from coercion.

This whole argument forces on me more and more the conviction that the fundamentals of social order depend on moral forces—conventions, habits, and ideals, mostly acquired from the social-cultural milieu—rather than on any framework of organizational structure or laws. In my next lecture I shall take up the ethics of the matter, what social ideals define progress and point the direction of desirable change, in so far as politically possible and feasible. There is no clear line between social necessity and the socially ideal. One might or might not say that it is necessary in itself not to let babies starve to death or die from lack of medical care; but the Greeks and others have practiced wholesale infanticide but had a high civilization. We know now that as regards many diseases health is a community affair, but also that a natural reproduction rate will soon lead to intolerable population pressure, if the babies grow up. How many are born and reared is not nearly so important for free society as it is that those who reach maturity have a necessary minimum of equipment for carrying the social responsibilities of membership in such a society. These responsibilities, economic, political and cultural, are indeed heavy—manifold greater than those imposed by pre-liberal static society. The people having been freed from any strict conformity to unchanging tradition, and from obedience to an established absolute authority, and having achieved or been given political equality for all normal adults, they are collectively responsible for the future of society and civilization. They must not only preserve order, and the level of culture inherited by a given generation from the past, but must also achieve progress. The future can no longer be left to the "slow and silent forces" of history. And even to hold a given level, a society must somehow keep its numbers in line with its resources, either by limiting the one or by expanding the other. The imperative of progress is inseparable from that of freedom, since freedom means freedom to make changes, and progress is to be achieved through freedom.

Changes will be in the direction either of improvement or deterioration; a literally stationary condition is hardly conceivable, and certainly impossible. Regardless of men's intentions, some changes will occur, and these will force the making of others—either intelligently, for the better, or else for the worse; for, the consequences of random or impulsive action, or action based on false judgments, will be predominantly bad. The first requisite for intelligent action is *knowledge,* particularly knowledge of the good, or ethical knowledge, the meaning of progress—and then knowledge of what is possible and how to achieve possible improvement. But the former is the hardest task; progress calls for constant redefinition of ideals as well as advance in the realization of those recognized at a given time and place. What I am calling ethical knowledge contrasts sharply with moral, though all knowledge is social; it is defined by agreement which, under freedom, is reached through free discussion, a cooperative quest of truth. Presupposed, of course, is a general *will* to learn, to agree, and a will to act on the best knowledge that is to be had.

Most directly in point here is agreement on the meaning of economic justice, and the nature of discussion to that end. The latter aspect will be a main topic for my final lecture. The issue of justice is acute especially because the natural tendency of individualistic economic behavior is in the direction of increasing inequality, through the use of economic means to acquire more such means; those who at any time have more are in a better position to get still more. But under realistic conditions very much inequality in this respect undermines the justice of exchange of equal market value contributions to output—and extreme inequality renders freedom of no effect. But that is a small part of the story. Recalling that individualism really means familism, this tendency does not cease to operate with the lives of any generation of acting individuals. Inequalities achieved—or resulting from good or bad "luck," which is a major factor and very hard to deal with or discuss—are passed on to the next generation. Inheritance of property is a major factor and hardly separable from the private family as an institution, but is by no means the only such factor, and at bottom doubtfully the most important. The ideal of no inherited inequality of status is impossible to realize. That theme must await later development. The fact of supreme importance is that inherited inequality entails an unequal start-in-life, which by the standards of individual ethics is palpably unfair.

What has just been said leads into the topics of the two remaining lectures of this series, dealing with the problems—especially the ethical problems—created by the liberation of the mind, or relation to its capacity for solving them. In conclusion here, I anticipate only with the reminder that it is basic human nature that has been liberated—the human mind, comprising feelings, intellect and will. This liberation, with political equality, gives rise to the distinctive and onerous problems of democratic society. In fact, these revolutionary changes have for the first time in history created genuinely social problems. These center in the responsibility for progress, to be combined with freedom, the absolute necessity of *order,* and also with minimum requirements of efficiency and justice, and individual security, and spiritual culture. That is, the essential problems lie in *conflicts* among these general norms. Ultimately, they are due to disharmonies in human nature, as it is, here and now, the product of evolution and history, or between human nature and the given conditions of life. How far or how fast either can be changed by deliberate action is then the ultimate problem for analysis, while the meaning of improvement or progress is its counterpart, calling for a critique of values.

Chapter V ~ THE ETHICS OF LIBERALISM

This lecture and the next, which will conclude the series, will not do much more than raise questions, offering little contribution to the answers. It has been said that fools ask questions and wise men answer them. If I'm a question asker rather than an answerer, my defense is to suggest that the first task of intelligence, and the hardest, is to ask the right questions. One requirement, indeed, is that a question must offer a fair chance of finding an answer worth the cost of the inquiry. But it is still true that many questions have to be answered, and will be, on extremely meager grounds, even practically at random.

To that indictment I must plead guilty, and also that of being better at criticizing other people's asking and answering than at doing either myself, and more addicted to the former role. But I have a defense, or two of them. First, I think the role fits in with the concept of democracy, that the function of the intellectual leader, in the difficult field of social philosophy and policy, is to clarify issues, or at most suggest possible solutions and perhaps arguments, pro and con. Answering is rather the task of Adam Smith's insidious and wily animal, the statesman or politician, which in a democracy means the ordinary citizen. A pointed illustration is the role of the jury in our administration of justice, in relation to the judge or expert witness. Secondly,

I suspect that the representative common-man is a better final authority on issues involving the weighing of basic values, than any individual whom there is a feasible way of selecting. Issues, that is, that are reasonably within his comprehension, and on which highly specialized knowledge and special techniques are not available or not applicable. I may say that in the three decades or so since I laboriously worked up a lecture on "The Ethics of Competition" (given at Harvard University and later published as an article in the *Quarterly Journal of Economics*—and still later reprinted in a book) I have done quite a lot of thinking about ethics and economics, and have perpetrated some wordage in print as well as in several university classrooms. As a result, I have become even more hesitant about speaking very definitely and positively.

There are so many approaches to these questions that an introduction needs to run well beyond the scope of a lecture. One approach to which I have become more and more attracted is the historical. What I want to say here about the ethics of liberalism ties directly onto my second lecture, on the historical background, especially the concept of the Liberal Revolution. What most impresses me, with regard to ethics in particular, is the general inversion of values, the radical change in Western man's view of himself and society in relation to the world effected by this cultural overturn. In which, we must bear in mind, the Industrial Revolution was a major factor, and back of that the modern scientific movement in its relation to applications in technology. Even the words we use have their history, and many have undergone a revolution in meaning; "ethics" itself, and others, will call for some defining as we go along. First, let me recall that "social action" is a new thing in history, essentially a product or an aspect of liberalism, and "intelligent" action in general in our instrumentalist meaning and as a subject of published discussion, is only a bit older. It was a product of modern applied science and was really brought to maturity in the development of economics. Action that is truly social is democratic action, that is, action not merely *for* a society but *by* society, with participation of its whole citizenry. "Freedom" also has radically changed its meaning; the history is too complex to go into here—but I must note that in my professional lifetime the meaning of its kindred term "liberalism" has been largely inverted. It used to signify individual liberty, and now means rather state paternalism. As I pointed out in an earlier lecture, freedom is *not* to be opposed to determinism, but to coercion, which is the term needing definition; and it is often misdefined as the opposite of "persuasion," which is clearly a form of coercion, perhaps the most important form.

Freedom is very commonly misdefined by making it include the *power* to do what one wants to do—which would practically call for omnipotence. In the metaphysical sense, the opposite of determinism, all choices are free; one chooses among the alternatives he finds open. Coercion consists in the arbitrary, and in general wrongful, use of power by one person to manipulate the alternatives of choice open to another. The major premise of liberal ethics is the right of every person to do as he will, without interference by any other—and as he *can,* or otherwise could. But in social life this right is subject to limitations. The first, which is self-evident if people generally are to be free, is that each must respect the same freedom on the part of others. Use of freedom to destroy freedom is a self-contradictory idea. Social problems arise in connection with further limitations, to be imposed on the individual by society, through its organs or agents. I stress *can* because that is where the major problem of definition arises—not, of course in the right to will any action. Freedom as a right presupposes, takes as given, both the means or power possessed by the person and what we may want to do. The latter factor hardly needs emphasis, since the wish is generally assumed—in fact much more than it ought to be—and in that connection freedom is misdefined only by over-stressing it, as the right and opportunity to do as one pleases. The whole idea of a right to freedom squarely inverts the preliberal (specifically medieval) doctrine of original sin (mentioned in Lecture II), the idea that if anyone does anything he wants to do he will do wrong, hence that people ought on principle to be restrained and directed by authority. In the Middle Ages there was no question about the omni-competent authority; it was the Roman Church, using the secular arm as its agent.

Freedom in society means, in short free (that is, voluntary) association, on terms freely agreed upon by the parties involved, in contrast with dictation by any prescriptive authority or law. The meaning and rightful limitations of this freedom are the matter chiefly to be discussed. The general limitation—respect by each of the same freedom in others— received a familiar statement by Herbert Spencer, though it is an old principle in modern law and social philosophy. Practically no one (the exception of a few anarchists may be neglected) questions the rightfulness or need of its enforcement by law and government, where this is required by the inadequacy of the conscience or intelligence of individuals. In the society of today—increasingly in the last generation or so—the task of government has become less that of preventing individuals from infringing on others' freedom than of inhibiting the activities or formation of groups organized for power—the pressure-groups mentioned in the preceding lecture. The major cases arise in economic relations, and have been discussed in connection with monopoly. The basic matter historically, the decisive factor in bringing on the Liberal Revolution—is the right to question currently accepted beliefs and patterns of conduct, established by custom and enforced by authority, and to promote changes. To that question the liberal answer is twofold, as already pointed out; it is a reasonable maximum of literal individual freedom and, where a social answer is necessary, it is to be reached through open discussion leading to agreement on some change or on non-change—agreement with a minimum of coercion. Human society is basically a phenomenon of more or less stable beliefs and patterns of conduct. The principle of liberalism is that these are not fixed once and for all—historically through prescription by some supernatural (or charismatic) authority—but are always subject to question, discussion, and alteration by agreement. Free society thus stands for progress, and also allows for and approves of much variety in both belief and conduct.

Associative life must be regulated by law—law in the imperative meaning in contrast with descriptive law, scientific or historical. In free society, to the extent that it is free, laws are made—changed and formulated through free discussion leading to agreement. But, human nature being as it is, discussion does not lead to unanimity on important issues, whence arises another major limitation on freedom; compulsion is involved in both law-making and its enforcement. The nearest a society gets to the ideal is "majority rule," itself an ideal which is rather remotely approximated in political reality. A society—its government—practically never acts in response to a majority opinion on an issue. Discussion of this matter would lead into the whole theory or democratic organization and action—how political representatives or agents are chosen and commissioned, given more or less limited delegated authority to act, and held more or less effectively responsible to a society as a whole. The scope of this lecture, or of the series, does not allow going into that in detail, but more will be said about it in the concluding lecture.

Our study, then, is finally of law; society is "law and order," terms that are close synonyms. Of course, all knowable reality is subject to law, in the scientific sense, and to historical laws. In that meaning there are legal relations and structures even in an animal society. Human society differs in having laws felt as normative, more or less imperative and compulsive, and subject to being broken, which as far as we know is not true of those regulating a bee-hive, a termite colony, or a flock or herd of a higher gregarious species. The root of it is the nature of human beings to have conflicting interests, conflicting between individuals and with social needs or requirements; and on these, individuals hold different opinions, and they by no means always do what they believe to be lawful or right. Thus arise social problems, in contrast with animal societies, where the laws are patterns of behavior (not conduct) inherited as instinct and presumably not consciously known. Original human society may have been equally unfree but determined on the different basis of "culture," a historical product inherited socially rather than biologically. In primitive society the laws are made by the forces of cultural history and evolution, as custom; but as far back as knowledge goes they had to be enforced, and societies developed various mechanisms to do that. Much later they developed ways of changing the laws, more or less, and more or less intelligently. But only in liberal society is this done "freely," by public discussion and rough agreement. If agreement were unanimous, there would be no laws, to be enforced, hardly even formally stated. Law and government must be more or less compulsory on individuals, or it would be superfluous, otiose.

Thus government by the people is, as already suggested, an ideal, not to say a somewhat figurative expression. In a democracy, laws are made (always meaning changed) by agents of the electorate, and are administered by other agents, both held more or less "responsible" by various devices, to their principal, the public. But all agents have more or less discretionary authority and power, and that is decidedly the case with legislators, and administrators and judges. Further, the more the society stresses freedom, mobility, change and variety, the more the functions of government are multiplied and elaborated, and the more it inevitably becomes in details a government by men and not of law. The latter ideal also can be less and less closely approximated, and the formula somewhat figurative. That is one of the dilemmas a democracy must face and must deal with by some compromise between freedom-and-progress and order—and incidentally, security. Much discretionary power is inevitable everywhere, and especially in political life—and perhaps even more in economic relations. As I noted in the preceding lecture, modern society is largely a tissue of agency relations; in consequence of specialization, especially of knowledge, some people make decisions for other people, and give them directions amounting to commands. I illustrated this in an ultra-simple case by the relations between a doctor and his patient, and the situation is much aggravated where an agent acts for a group instead of an individual. These facts create a new type of moral problem. In pre-liberal society—medieval Western Europe an extreme example, where authorities were "responsible to God"—the problems were entirely different and vastly more limited. Even there, the laws were in part made by men, since a law must be interpreted, hence is what some constituted authority says it is, and execution cannot be entirely separated from law-making. The established authority must be obeyed until it is changed, or the law is changed, or both. Depending on the constitution and the facts of the situation, laws may be changed by authoritative fiat or by rebellion, which of course ends the rule of law and of the previous authority, until new ones become established—if they ever do—if the society survives. In a democracy, they are normally changed by discussion and orderly process prescribed by law itself—finally constitutional law, which normally provides for its own amendment. But democracies are also subject to insurrection and civil war. And it needs to be stressed that that possibility of changing the law, even by war or a dictator, is limited. Basically, law is the *mores,* which in other fields are more or less like a language and its laws, little amenable to voluntary change. However, the power of a dictatorship to change even quite fundamental laws has lately been shown to be surprisingly wide—disappointingly so, for those cherishing democratic ideals.

The concrete individual freedoms requiring limitation and regulation by law consist chiefly of two groups. First, there is economic cooperation, organized through the free exchange of goods and services in free markets. Not all such cooperation is so organized, however; exchange may take place on any other terms than market prices on which the parties may agree, more or less freely or subject only to persuasion. This is an aspect of the free-enterprise economy needing constant emphasis: that any who object to the market organization are free to adopt any other on which they can secure agreement by the other parties concerned— which involves mixing gift with exchange, as long as the market organization sets the accepted standards of value. Secondly, we group together innumerable other voluntary associations, often lost sight of by undue concentration of attention on what are called economic problems. These extend from casual conversation and social parties and clubs to groupings for cultural pursuits. Especially important in modern society are various manifestations of the play interest —games and sports, which actually permeate both our economic and our political life. (As I have said before, both politics and economics are as much competitive games as they are instrumentalities for meeting recognized needs or satisfying wants.) And, of course, religion. In the prescriptive type of society religion is dominant. In a free society it must be another example of free association, to the extent that society is free. So far as it is organized at all and not purely a personal matter with the individual, it must be free association. Free society is inevitably a secular society, since men will not agree freely on supernatural truth. Adherents of any one religion must be tolerant of other religious views if peace and order and freedom are to prevail. Religion opposes progress, as men will not accept or worship a God who changes his mind and his laws. In a free society there cannot be any such thing as sacred truth, or any dogma or matter which is not open to question and to change; and thereby arise problems of boundless complexity and difficulty.

All *free* discussion is finally discussion of values. That is, it is a cooperative effort to achieve truth—truth is tested by agreement—about values, the desirable things, reached by weighing evidence. Ideal values must be distinguished from wishes or desired things, and both the desirable and the desired must be distinguished from facts, in the ordinary use of that word. Yet both desires and values are facts, in different senses. Desires exist in individual minds, and normative values have objective validity; they are not purely personal. Mere assertion of an opinion can only intensify disagreement; it can never lead to that agreement on which social order is predicted. Truth must be distinguished from opinion and especially from wishful opinions, "prejudices," which to my mind is the heart of the problem of agreement, rather than honest error or ignorance. Truth is a value and in a sense the all-inclusive value. We assume that the other values in the familiar triad—Beauty, or Good Taste, and the Good—also have truth. This comes up here because, as I will stress, ethics in the sense in which it has to do with social policy includes all the values which enter into civilization and into the guidance of social opinions and actions. The distinctions among this famous triad—the True, the Beautiful, and the Good—can never be clear. One can hardly be defined so as not to include the other two. I illustrate with respect to truth and beauty by the famous poetic utterance of Keats about their identity. "Beauty is truth and truth beauty. That is all we know and all we need to know." The statement demonstrates its own falsity, since it is itself beautiful but not true. But the confusion between the True and the Good is more fundamental. The Good also includes all values: Good, for the purpose of deciding on any major social policy, includes everything that enters into a high civilization, and into progress. The general objective is good conduct of good men in a good society, which spells out as simply improving civilization. I have been impressed and a little depressed by the difficulty of finding serious discussion of what people mean by the phrase, used so freely, of a high or higher civilization. What are the criteria by which we judge a civilization? These will obviously include Truth, Beauty, and Goodness or justice—and refinement, fun, humor, and all the other values which people recognize as entering into the good life, many of which were not recognized at all in the religious morality of the Middle Ages, in the prescriptive type of society. Economic efficiency to provide the necessary means of all life was particularly ignored, even treated scornfully.

The Good means the better; there is no such thing as a meaningful ideal of perfection. Ideals themselves are subject to improvement as they are approached, and there is no ultimate goal. As near as we can formulate any concept or description of the good society, it will certainly include a great variety of individuals and, in the world or in any large area, a great variety of societies, too. No specific organization form can ever be valid. In science, obviously, there is no goal, there is no *the* Truth; conceptually, there is only the better view, as is more clearly the case with other validities. I have mentioned that the beginning of the idea of progress was the questioning of cosmic or astronomical truth by Copernicus and Galileo. We have gone on to the general recognition that there is no such thing as finality in science, and this idea tends to spread—but much more slowly than it should—into the other fields where it should be self-evident. For it is even more true that there is no such thing as finality in the idea of good social order or good laws.

The second main consequence of the liberal revolution is that all truth is provisional, all knowledge and all valuations relative. The concept of truth is progressive, dynamic. The main reason law and authority are necessary is that people as citizens, as members of society, disagree on fundamental values: I do not think they usually seriously violate standards they recognize as right. But man is a disagreeing animal, an opinionated animal, conceited, prejudiced, dogmatic and addicted to regarding his opinions as sacred or absolute. It is no marvel that, prior to the liberal epoch, only a century or two preceding our own, the basis of society had to be sacred truth and a sacred pattern of action, consequently absolute, varying, and universal. The Deity does not change his mind. I have said that the whole problem of beauty and taste is very much neglected in this connection, although there is plenty written about it as an independent problem. But esthetic disagreement does not often create a serious social problem. More important for our purpose is the tendency to confuse truth with goodness, to moralize and then to take a religious view of both truth and right, to hold that they are absolutely sacred dogma—not open to question. This would be my definition of religious belief: any belief held as absolute on moral grounds, so that to question it is wicked. Before the liberal epoch, that was *the* meaning of *truth*, the German *Treue*, trust, or fidelity—rather than intellectual validity or cogency. Preliberal society is a moral and religious social order, and this view tends to survive into our liberal cultures, where it has no place, in the form of dogmatism and intolerance. Man is still inveterately a moralizing animal. I am sure that originally the ordinary meaning of "why" as explanation is "who is to blame,"—or exceptionally "who is to be praised," exceptionally because it is usually the bad things that need explanation. This view still permeates our linguistic usage and even our feeling attitudes.

There can be no truth which is not open to question; but discretion must be used—very great discretion—as to what questions are raised and discussed; for human individual attention is very limited and the possible scope of discussion is enormously more limited still. Here is one of the problems for which there cannot be any formal answer: what questions are worth discussing? In general, we can only take one at a time, which on the whole means a tiny fraction of the boundless number that might be found and gone into, and there can be no adequate handling of those. The most important of our laws are laws regulating discussion, the Rules of Order. For discussion itself, laws have to be made by discussion, but that discussion has to be regulated by law, and these laws, too, have to be administered by an authority with a good deal of discretionary power. We face this anomalous and perhaps somewhat vicious circle of law and authority governing the discussion that makes laws and selects authorities. Furthermore, discussion is necessarily limited to those persons who are to some degree capable of it. Another main field and necessity of law is to limit the circle of discussion. Freedom of discussion—or any other freedom for that matter—has absolutely no meaning for infants. Society as a legal entity must take much responsibility and exercise much compulsion in the interest of its children, in the form of education and of support. This is one of the main limitations of the Spencerian definition of freedom, which assumes that society is made up of responsible individuals, a view that is absurdly contrary to fact. At least two of F. D. Roosevelt's four freedoms are also absurd: "freedom from" want and "freedom from" fear.

Society is not made up of given, responsible individuals.

There is a lot of nonsense in political discussion due to not recognizing, first of all, the fact that "men" are men, women, and children—with further subdivisions. This makes a vast difference from the standpoint of citizenship, as to rights and duties. Fitness for responsibility is not a matter of all-or-none but is a matter of degree. The law must decide who are to be participants in political discussion—that is, active citizens. First of all, of course, some age of maturity must be set by a more of less arbitrary rule. Then, some rules must be made and administered as to the mental and moral competence of those who are adult in physiological age. There is a basic fallacy in the whole idea of society as individualistic in any literal sense, as I have said before. What is called individualism should be called familism, and a most crucial freedom is freedom of family life. People have rights by virtue of being born into a particular society, in particular the freedom to marry and produce new units, with little effective responsibility for them afterwards. But this freedom conflicts with social interests and becomes a serious and ultimately a crucial matter. It is a self-evident truth that if a society is to maintain any sort of standards, there has to be some way of maintaining a workable relation between the number of people to be supported and the means of support. Again, religious traditions loom up in this connection. I remember a statement made by Henry Wallace that every baby in the world has a right to its bottle of milk: that is morally very appealing, but the traditional policy of organized Christianity has been in the direction of more babies and fewer bottles of milk.

All the way through, the extreme contrast between the religiously grounded society and the liberal society is the thing that it seems to me needs emphasis, particularly from

the ethical point of view. Liberalism has radically trans-
formed the whole idea and problem of the "good" as a
practical issue. Our free society evolved, or burst forth quite
suddenly in historical terms from the un-free society of
medieval Western Europe, which was an extreme form of
the typical primitive society through the ages. Prior to
liberalism and where it is not yet established, the right or
the "just" is defined by accord with the law, viewed as given,
eternal, and immutable, supernaturally ordained and supernaturally sanctioned, and interpreted by an authority with
the same attributes. The authority in the medieval Western
World was, of course, the officials of the Church of Rome.
The Church also claimed the unlimited right to legislate
as well as to interpret and enforce the divine law, but in
general it acted on the very different claim of merely administering a supernaturally given unalterable law into
action. Premises of that sort inevitably define, in essence, a
society based on a caste system. The individual is born into
a social status or position in life in which it is his duty to
live out his life—in theory, to work out his salvation. Each
individual had to work out his destiny, his lot, in the station
of life in which he was born. This was not seriously affected
by the fact that the supreme caste—the priesthood—was
based on co-option rather than birth.

What connection did this medieval social order have with
Christianity? We find two main Christianities in the New
Testament Gospels, with the Pauline writings more or less
in between: first, the ethical teachings of the synoptic
gospels, chiefly Matthew and Luke, which we usually have
in mind when the phrase "Christian ethics" is used; and
second, the very different view of the gospel of John, in
which Christianity is made a gospel of redemption akin to

numerous other mystery cults of salvation prevalent in that region before Christianity appeared. Christianity also took up the Jewish tradition of a Messiah, a deliverer-king, along with the conception of Deity as a God of righteousness. None of the main Christianities had anything in particular to do with the medieval authoritarian ecclesiasticism, and the last was related to liberalism as a background against which it arose as a reaction. History reveals a kind of third law of motion in social affairs in which an extreme position provokes a reaction, and the medieval relapse from classical civilization was such an extreme, tending to swing far in the opposite direction. I think, as I said in the first lecture, that the change that finally led to modernism began historically with the heresies, themselves reactionary not liberal, advocating a revolt against the imperialism of the papacy and a movement back toward a spiritual religion something like what had been taught by Jesus and the apostles as pictured in the record.

The liberal society that ultimately emerged has as its ideal, first of all, equality before the law; hereditary status—which is an inevitable feature of a static society, and particularly of a static society with a religious foundation—is in principle repudiated and as far as possible abolished. Equality before the law means that there is equal opportunity for everyone to find or make his own place in society. This ideal was dishonored in the breach rather than honored in the observance for some time into the age of liberalism, notably by this country in the matter of racial discrimination. We were from a generation to a century behind the main civilized world in getting rid of slavery nominally based on race, but actually a caste distinction, and then had to do it by one of the most terrible wars in history. We still do not allow equal legal treatment, but discriminate on the fictitious ground of any supposed trace of alien racial blood.

The ideal of strictly equal opportunity regardless of birth is again impossible. To take it literally is to fly in the face of unalterable facts. Under the family system, or indeed any reasonably conceivable substitute, the position into which one is born must inevitably go a long way toward determining the position in which one will live and the character of the life open to him. The hardest problem of social justice arises not in adjusting relations between contemporary living individuals, but in constructing relations between the generations. Our laws have not only to adjudicate existing conflicts of interest, but also to provide for the unborn and deal with the future character of civilization. In this, distributive justice in economic life is one of the important details, and is probably the source of the greatest amount of contemporary controversy and political turmoil.

The problem has no definite solution. We have to recognize at least three or four conceptions of economic justice which are partly harmonious and partly conflicting. If they were simply conflicting, the problem would be a good deal simpler than it is, in that it would call for a choice, not compromise and combination. Remembering that at a given time, the issue in free society is a matter of relations between persons and not justice defined by a given law known to all, based on a divinely ordained structure of social status, we get the first ideal of distributive justice: that each person should share in the social product according to his contribution to it. Even scripture warns that what a man soweth, that shall he also reap. If there were time for economic analysis, it would show that this is what results from market freedom and rational individual behavior. The free economy tends to give each individual participant a share in the joint output measured by his contribution to the total. On the other hand, this criterion has extremely little ethical significance in idealistic terms, since what people contribute is limited by what they are in a position to contribute, and that depends on their capacities. But their capacities—labor power or property owned—and their dispositions too, are in a large part derived from the social process, for which they are not to be held responsible. A second ideal, familiar in discussion, is distribution according to need. This principle is appealing and has to be taken into account very largely but, like the other, it cannot be erected into a single universal norm of distributive justice because there could never conceivably be any general agreement on the details, on measuring needs, or how they would be met. Distribution on the basis of productive contribution has moral claims too, and in addition is the mechanism by which production is organized and motivated, and without effective production there is nothing to distribute. A self-contained group cannot get very far away from this principle; it has to live on the product as a group, over any considerable period of time. It does not have to live every day on that day's product, but averaging out over no very long periods, what is consumed must be limited to what is produced, with allowance for maintenance and growth of productive capacity. In addition we have to have increasing production to provide for any rise in the standard of living or even to maintain the same standard for a growing population. Within the group, some departure from the productive contribution basis is possible, in favor of other norms. Third, there is the principle of equality: share and share alike. This is the principle of "unto this last," on which Ruskin wrote a book, taking the phrase from one of the parables in the New Testament. Finally, there is a fourth principle, which is advocated a good deal by particular prospective beneficiaries; it is that of rewards in accord with the dignity of the calling or of the individual: honor to whom honor is due, and so on. That is, it is supposed to be fitting in some absolute sense for members of the learned professions, especially, to have a higher standard of living than those who perform the more menial occupations. Obviously, the exact opposite could be cogently argued: since these genteel and interesting activities are to a considerable extent their own reward, those who live by them should be content with a smaller share of the material fruits of action rather than demanding a larger share.

What to do about all this is a problem for legal action. The realm of law is much larger than that of government and what is called "jural" law, enforced and to some extent made by officials. Morals and manners and those habitual patterns of which men are largely or wholly unconscious are after all the main framework of order within which laws enacted and enforced operate on a fairly narrow fringe. Manners are the greater part of morals, and the moral sentiments of a community are the foundation of its laws in the jural sense.

From the standpoint of social philosophy, the categorical difference made in the social order by the liberal revolution, establishing the principle of freedom and individual responsibility and social responsibility for the future, is the shift of problems from the field of morals—in the proper original sense of *mores*, here considered apart from any religious sanctioning—to that of intelligence. That is, as I propose to use the words, a shift from morals to ethics, the only word that seems to be available for a necessary distinction between traditional and given norms and the more inclusive and dynamic, forward-looking, value problems involved in envisaging and attempting to secure progress, to build a better society through a better system of laws. The great difference, of course, the revolutionary difference, is that in a static society—and I refer to the Middle Ages in Western Europe as a type—people know what is "right." They learn what "is done," and what is to be done, as they learn to talk, and do it as naturally, without agony or compulsion about it. Choices in such a situation are "moral"—we have no other words to express what I want to say here; that is, they are choices between "right" and "wrong." They are a matter of will and not of intellectual deliberation and decision.

In a progressive society the opposite is the case; people need a vast amount of knowledge to act intelligently in their social capacity as citizens. They need to predict the consequences of action and to judge rightly between those of any proposed change and inaction, letting events take their natural course—an ethical judgment. They have to have fairly accurate knowledge and must learn through laborious and patient effort. People incline to snap judgments, or take too much for granted. Education is practically a problem distinctive of a liberal society, which must have an educated public, able and willing to bear its responsibilities.

In primitive society people know what they need to know, almost as animals know what to do in the situations they meet with. They learn it automatically, with the exception of very special roles, chiefly the medicine man or whatever the religious functionary may be or be called. In a free society everyone should know a lot of things that nobody can ever know very accurately, and they have to come to an agreement on them. This calls for a vast amount of tolerance, after much laborious effort. This knowledge is not a matter of logic or scientific induction; the two things which we have especially to know in order to act intelligently are history, including events and their causes, and ethics as I am talking about it here: the system of values that enables us to discriminate between the better and the worse in contemplating action with a view to changing the nature of society. These are matters of critical judgment, and as far as I can see there is no definite methodology for the discussion of values. It depends more on will and innate faculty and disposition than it does on any techniques that could ever be formulated into rules. As a matter of fact, I myself do not take too much stock in methodology in the natural sciences as being useful to the investigator; and even though it may be meaningful there, I doubt that there is anything at all comparable in the study of social philosophy and political ethics.

I have been raising questions to which I, at least, do not see the answers—questions which, with the common attitudes toward them, frankly seem to justify doubts about the future of free society. If it is to survive society itself must manage somehow to work a very considerable change in human nature as it has come down into this liberal epoch from some half million years of previous human history in comparison with which the liberal epoch is a few minutes on the clock. That question—the question whether human nature has what it takes to solve the problems which have been raised by its liberation—is the topic announced for the next and final discourse in this series.

Chapter VI ~ CAN THE MIND SOLVE THE PROBLEMS RAISED BY ITS LIBERATION?

"Human nature" is the subject to be studied for an understanding of what goes on in society and for designing measures for improvement. It must be considered in two aspects, the problems it raises and its capacity for dealing with them. More intelligence is needful in both respects. It must be kept in mind that the human nature now existing is the product of a long evolution, under conditions radically different from those of our free-and-progressive society—and with largely antithetical requirements. Moreover, free society, with its liberal world-view, burst into history very recently and suddenly, in historical terms, through a profound cultural revolution. Previously, and notably in medieval Western Europe (a little way back in our historical background) society was ruled by customary law that had grown rather than been made, and was not thought subject to substantial change. The need was for conformity in conduct and belief; this called in practice for obedience to an interpreting authority in both fields, not for intelligent initiative. The essence of the revolution was replacement of conformity and obedience by the antithetical couplet, freedom and progress; the result was problems that did not exist before, for individuals and especially for the social collectivity.

We recall that the revolution took place in two general

stages, at, respectively, the Renaissance, and the Enlighten-ment. The first stage effected two major changes. One was to transfer the supreme authority from "The Church" to "states" under absolute monarchs ruling by divine-right. The other was destruction by a new scientific movement—with respect to physical phenomena—of belief in eternal and immutable knowledge, specifically as supernaturally re-vealed. Biology was later added to the field so affected (in fact well after the Enlightenment). The second stage was important for extending to morals and law the area subject to intelligent change through new knowledge. This was associated, as cause and effect, with political democratization, and introduced genuinely social problems. The situation of the individual in a free-and-progressive society contrasts sharply with that of a "static" culture. In the latter, a normal adult will naturally know what is right—learned as he learns the spoken language—and confronts only the moral choice between right and wrong. (The latter was sin, since preliberal social order was viewed as divinely ordained and sanctioned.) The general result of the liberation was to replace the injunction "be good," in a conventional or sentimental sense, with "be intelligent" or "be good intelli-gently."

However, the Enlightenment ideas in this field exhibited a "pendular" reaction, going to extremes in the opposite direction. They embodied a romantically exaggerated con-ception of human reason, reasonableness and good will—the antithesis of the doctrine of original sin, previously held as sacred truth. Logically carried through, as some writers practically did, the social implication would be anarchism. This would also exclude real problems, for, the individual would not only know the right but would spontaneously do it. The main field in which the doctrine of freedom was carried to excess in practice was economic relations, particularly in Britain, which, with its North American colonies (in a somewhat different role) became the milieu in which liberalism developed. Fully on a par with the establishment of representative political institutions was the adoption of economic *laisser faire,* recognizing the virtual independence of the market-and-enterprise organization, which had been growing up since the Middle Ages (and at this time received a major impetus from the Industrial Revolution).

Overdoing this policy soon led to a reaction, beginning with the first Factory Acts. The breakdown came in the field of the employment of children (and in part of women) under scandalous conditions, that is, where it was "stupid" to think of individual responsibility as applicable in the first place. From that beginning, the reaction has spread, and during and since the nineteenth century the relations between the state and the economic order have become the major problem of political action and controversy. Much of what has occurred, intelligence should have foreseen and could in part have forestalled. But disillusionment is not yet complete, and, on the other hand, while much of the reaction itself, in the form it has taken, cannot be described as intelligent. Our title involves the relation between the problem-raising and the problem-solving components of human nature; and the "liberation of the mind" seems to have released a tendency to acute discontent, criticism, fault-finding that was there all along but held in check by the harsh discipline of preliberal culture—or possibly new conditions have caused it to develop with astonishing speed as a culture trait. Conditions that might so operate are only too easy to think of, and speculation about them must be omitted here. I propose to deal only with the real and serious problems that necessarily arise out of freedom—but recognize, of course, that there would be much difference of opinion about the selection. Another matter that can only be named and stressed is the relation between problem-solving capacity and the will to use it, or use it intelligently.

An embarrassment I have referred to before is the fact that discussion of social problems comes down so largely to self-evident propositions; it is hard to get beyond these and one does not get far beyond before running into real issues that are insoluble and very difficult to treat significantly in brief compass. By self-evident I mean obviously true, not false, as in the connection most familiar hereabouts—proclaiming that men are born equal and divinely endowed with various rights. It is illuminating to reflect that the famous Declaration emanated from slave-holders and was set forth on behalf of a nation that, in part, maintained slavery for nearly a century. I constantly feel an impulse to apologize for the triteness of most of what can be said. The first commandment, with respect to any intelligent action is self-evident: "compare the alternatives," beginning with understanding what they are. But that is what people dislike doing. And the second and third are, appraise the alternatives, and then act on the basis of the best knowledge or judgment that is to be had. The basic axiom is that it is better not to act unless it can be done intelligently; as people are and as the world is, the odds are strong that bad results on balance, rather than good, will follow from acting ignorantly, at random—and acting on false knowledge is of course worse; but unhappily it is more common.

The next step is to note a few obvious facts about the knowledge required for intelligent action, particularly group action, indicating the limitations of the knowledge possessed or probably obtainable. Any human subject, individual or group, to act intelligently must have knowledge under some four headings. Moved by a sense of a difference between some situation as it is and as he would like it to be in the future, an individual must first know what he can do that might effect some change. Next (the order of listing is arbitrary) he must know the consequences that will or would follow from any such possible act. This covers two items— knowledge of the "natural" course of events, as it will (or would) be in the absence of any action, and the difference to be expected from any act, in comparison with not-acting. Finally, he must appraise and judge among all these consequences (of action and inaction) and choose the "best" alternative open. Under all headings knowledge and the possibility of knowledge adequate for rational behavior are limited.

The first calls for knowing one's own capacities, including the properties of all instruments and materials available for use—in short, technology in that inclusive meaning. The assumption of a given technology is necessary for economic analysis at the stage dealing with the stationary conditions, a valid and indispensable concept, but no one pretends that it is very realistic. Rigidly interpreted, it would mean a behavioristic view of behavior, which contradicts the idea of economizing activity—but does not mean that has no place in analysis.

The second and third headings call for predictive knowledge. Under the second, the substance would consist of historical laws governing (as we say—in reality describing) sequences of events, while the third heading adds knowledge of the kind provided by the natural sciences that are instrumental to action. That means hypothetical laws, stating what will happen if a particular event occurs, which is assumed to be contingent—in our case the immediate change introduced by the action of our subject. A few sciences—astronomy is the type—can predict unconditionally, what will actually happen at a given place and a given future date. The more familiar kinds of science cannot do that, where human intervention is involved, because in general the human act is unpredictable. That is the case even in a laboratory, where the human act is to conduct an experiment; and likewise holds for all technology. Prediction by a subject of his own behavior is methodologically a very different matter from predicting that of anyone else, and both differ radically from predicting natural nonhuman events. In all the human cases, discoverable historical and scientific laws answer our questions to a quite limited extent and no method or combination of methods yields at all accurate or reliable results. Thus in general it is possible to predict only where there is no chance to do anything about the phenomena (the case of astronomy) but the converse does not hold; an individual's power to predict the behavior of his own society is drastically restricted, in spite of his negligible power of control. Biological evolution, and especially the weather, are examples of natural phenomena of which the same is largely true. Unconditional prediction is useful only for adapting conduct to the given conditions in question.

The general issue opened up by considering the third division of knowledge is the possibility of a social science in the relevant meaning, as predictive of the consequences of social action. What has been said so far is relevant chiefly for intelligent individual activity aimed at redirecting the course of natural events. It has little application to social action, because of radical differences in the nature of the problem. Even in the former field, its significance is highly abstract, since in ordinary reality action upon nature is in the main social action and, even more important, conscious human knowledge is itself a social phenomenon, a mode of social action. The situation of a Crusoe is useful for bringing out certain very general principles of individual motivation, but must assume an adult brought up in a human-social milieu, if it is not to be too unrealistic even for that purpose. Before going further into social science, it is requisite to glance at the fourth species of knowledge, that of the ends of action, which presents the major difficulties of the general problem, and here the Crusoe hypothesis can be illuminating. Analysis of motivated behavior (conduct) typically assumes that an individual knows the answer to the question raised under this head—that is, knows intuitively or from unsystematic experience his degrees of preference among alternatives to be considered. The matter would be comparatively simple for a Crusoe, since he would hardly be concerned with moral values, or anything but his own subjective preferences. More in doubt is taste, as affected by a sense of imperative, or objective norms. That also may be passed over here, but it is still unrealistic to assume that individual preferences present no problem to the acting subject, in looking to the future. They would probably call for considerable "deliberation"; but there seems to be little to say about a general pattern, or methodology. Quite certainly, some systematic, primitively scientific investigation would be carried on by a Crusoe in learning what he "could" do to and with various objects and features in his environment. But such details have only negative relevance here.

The main fact for our present inquiry is that knowledge,

especially for social action, is social knowledge; it depends on and is practically defined by agreement. Even scientific knowledge of nature must be *verified*, or taken on faith as verifiable. But the nub of the social-action problem is the necessity of agreement upon ends, and the primary general end is some change in society itself and its members. Society is both the actor and the matter to be acted upon. I must pass over the problem, important as it is, of the individual member in relation to his society; his need for predicting its future has been mentioned, and this would lead into the effort to change it by individually instrumental action. The ideal of mutual freedom, strictly interpreted, excludes such action, in favor of democratic discussion, which is the matter for discussion here. The general objective is simply the continuous improvement of society, its organization and its membership, or social *progress*.

Looking again at the four heads or species of knowledge, the first task is to predict the future as the course of events to be expected in the absence of action. Taken literally and strictly, this project hardly makes sense; it cannot be separated from that of the consequences of "possible" action, and the action a society can take on itself is another matter so vague that not much that is at all definite can be said about it in general terms. Unquestionably, a society can change its constitution and laws, which is the general nature of social action. The question is, *what* changes are possible? and the answer is a matter of separating the "inevitable" course of history from the factors subject to change by intelligent action. In a word it is the problem of *history*; and what can or cannot be done to affect *predictably* the future course of social history must be considered with reference to fairly concrete proposals for action. What can be done is again almost entirely a matter of reaching agreement on what it is desirable to do, and what not to do, that is, on the objective, the kind of society to be projected for the future. (The idea of complete inaction, by a free society or any human individual, surely does not make sense at all.) This is true of society as an organic entity. What a society can do by organized action to change its members is another question of supreme importance but so difficult that little can be said about it. The prior question is also very real and must be faced. A large and fundamental part of the course of events is clearly not subject to voluntary and intelligent change; an example is the spoken language. Again, it can hardly be said that if a society was in agreement on a desirable change, it could not be affected; but the case of (English) spelling reform is convincing evidence of the practically insuperable difficulty. Other features or elements of usage in conduct and in beliefs and attitudes are in every degree like or unlike language in this respect. (I have previously mentioned the imperative need for improvement in the medium of communication, especially for a common language for the civilized world; but practical action seems to be hopelessly outside the area of useful discussion.)

Intelligent control of the future course of history is *the* problem, and action is constantly being taken to that end, if indeed it is not the nature of all social action undertaken. The problem is so complex and difficult that little can be said about methodology or procedure looking to its solution. Only a few generalizations can be offered here, chiefly in the negative way of pointing out the obvious difficulties, but with some indication of qualifications of these which keep them from being entirely insuperable and the problem hopeless. Some common errors in thinking can at least be pointed out, as a contribution to better analysis, which is a first requisite for any effective action. An error that is perhaps not crucially important practically, except for causing wasted effort and needless controversy, is any attempt to define a goal of social progress in any specific or final sense. The concept of perfection in human affairs is without meaning and should be banished from serious discourse. Any goal must be highly provisional and subject to change at any time, regardless of advance toward its realization. The best society to be envisaged will always comprise infinitely complex congeries of societies, made up of an infinite variety of individual members, more or less good in relation to their roles and the standards for judgment—and all constantly in a flux of change. (It is significant that the commonly pictured supreme end of life, Heaven, is the precise antithesis.)

Another point worth noting is that most discussion of the problem of history has been centered on the role of individuals—the hero—an implicit contrast with historical forces, but without much effort to find usable laws. Attributing significant influence to individuals is again contrary to the nature of the ideal democratic process as cooperative discussion. However, the vital part that must be played by individuals in any realistically possible society, as leaders, and possessing authority and power, will presently call for consideration and emphasis.

Enough has been said to make it clear that thinking about social action and the knowledge in question cannot be "scientific," in at all the instrumental meaning of the scientific technology through which man exercises control over nature. The major question is that of ends, that is, of agreement on these; the procedure is instrumental in the broad sense of acting so as to achieve an objective; but this is not an end, and still less does the action involve the use of means in anything like the way in which physical objects and materials are used as means in engineering technology. An existing social order is to be used for its own improvement, but that is not properly a means-end relation. Moreover, constitutional details are of secondary importance. The legal framework of any existing formally democratic, responsible, government, is fairly adequate, if intelligently used—without any revolution or major change not provided for in the constitution itself. The hard problem, to repeat, is discussion of ends, leading to agreement, which will presently be taken up at greater length. The primary consideration for democracy, is *free* agreement; the conclusion actually reached is secondary—up to the point where there is a threat of outright destruction or an insurrection putting an end to freedom. The discussion is fundamentally about values, which must be treated as objective, excluding (again) the instrumental attitude in terms of individual ends. Issues arise out of conflicts of interest, which must take the form of differences of opinion. The mere assertion of opposed interests can only exacerbate the conflict and incite appeal to force.

Another approach incompatible with intelligent freedom is the religious, including magic and appeal to supernatural powers—the difference between the two being more formal or metaphysical than substantive or practical. Enough has perhaps been said about religion in earlier lectures. It has played two sharply contrasting roles—superstitious fear has served to secure conformity to a static law (through obedience to an interpreting authority) and it often develops into a procedure for salvation, that is, escape from the responsibilities of life into a mystical or supermundane realm of some sort. The incompatibility with free and intelligent action is obvious with respect to both.

The values in question are moral values, in a broad interpretation—with an important distinction to be noted in a moment. They are conduct values, or more specifically social relations in conduct, including relations in and between groups formally organized and acting as units. In the main the serious conflicts arise between groups rather than individuals. The groups present an infinite complexity, partly a hierarchical order from the family as the smallest effective unit up to sovereign states, and beyond those, the world, which conditions increasingly require to be a social order of some kind. The term "moral" is inadequate and misleading for the values in question in a free-and-progressive society, where the issues center in change in ideals themselves far more than achievement of given ideals. To have a distinctive term for progressive morality, the word "ethics" might serve, instead of being used as a close synonym for morals. The latter would then be kept for its original and etymological meanings, the *mores,* or customary usages and standards; there is already some distinction in meaning between the two words, in some conformity with this suggestion.

Ethical values, then, or moral values in a broad interpretation will refer to social improvement, or progress, as indicated before. It will mean a conservative liberalism, two words commonly used for contrasting political positions—but the only defensible difference is a fairly narrow one of emphasis. Some division must of course be made in emphasis and in the use of resources, between preserving the fruits of previous progress and making further improvement. But the range of intelligent choice is not wide; the danger is going to extremes in either direction, or especially in the present climate of opinion, making actions with too little regard for consequences. (I referred in an earlier lecture to the inversion of meaning of "liberalism"—from the policy of maximum liberty to state paternalism.) Assuming that our society is intelligently dedicated to freedom, the problem in the concrete becomes that of a right relation between this and other values, when and as they come into conflict with it. The absolute priority belongs to *order,* with "law" as a synonym; that is the essence of society, and in comparison, freedom is a luxury. The question is, how much order—no one wants society put in a straitjacket—and what kind. More concretely, it is, how much law and what laws are desirable, in the jural sense of laws with provision for enforcement. That depends not only on social ideals but on these in relation to what human nature will do if too much freedom is allowed. A third value to be named is *security,* but it is practically a corollary of order, and raises the same problems of how much, and what kind, in detail.

Another absolute requirement is *efficiency* in the use of resources—in achieving whatever balance of ends is agreed upon as the best possible. This calls for a workable and effective economic organization, providing for conservation and progress. Production must be increased if the level of life is to be improved—or even to maintain an initial level with increasing population. It is self-evident that if any standard is to prevail, above the natural level of savagery or brute life, numbers must somehow be kept down accordingly, and well below what is natural under any higher standard, specifically if there is action dealing with disease and famine. A fifth value to be listed separately is *progress,* though its content is defined by other values. And a sixth is *justice,* actually the most controversial of all. It is self-evident that a free society must approach general agreement on the meaning of distributive as well as criminal justice, and achieve at least a close enough approximation to some acceptable ideal to avoid disorder that would destroy freedom—or conceivably a deliberate rejection of free institutions in favor of some authoritarian control expected by the masses to better meet their demands. Finally to be specified is "culture," asthetic and intellectual, and progress in that respect.

Social action concretely viewed consists primarily in enforcing law; to this, freedom-and-progress add the vastly harder problem of making law, that is, changing the laws, since there always are laws. The added task also makes this a social problem in the real sense, since under stationary conditions decisions are moral rather than intellectual—including even those to be made by the law-enforcing authority. In discussing problems of law, in the intellectual atmosphere of our culture, conditioned by science and technology, we tend to use the terminology of means-and-means, philosophically misleading as it has just been shown to be. But sound thinking is instrumental in the sense that action is to be directed to producing a predicted and desired result—in this case the desirable one of social progress. Enforcement is the function of criminal procedure, broadly defined, though in primitive society most of the crimes or misdemeanors recognized in modern European law were technically "torts," crime consisting chiefly of religious offenses. (And in general there is no clear division between civil and criminal liability.) Further, the difference between punishment and exchange may fade into a psychological distinction. Punishment may be a fine; and culprits subjected to a fine, or even a mild prison sentence, have been known to view the penalty as the price paid for a privilege, and to say that it was worth the cost.

The most important field of social action in the current scene, that which bulks largest, and occasions by far the most controversy, is that of relations between the state as law and government and the market-and-enterprise organization of economic life. The problem is primarily moral, in the broad interpretation of progressive morals or ethics, and centers especially in economic or distributive justice. The most concrete issues have been considered in the previous lectures on the economic order and on the ethics of liberalism. I have already stressed that all serious social problems relate to conflicts between fundamental values, which are traditionally classified under the three heads of Truth, Beauty, and the Good, or intellectual, esthetic, and moral—the latter needing to be expanded into "ethics." I have also observed that the classification is logically vague, that the classes are neither homogeneous nor mutually exclusive. In fact, each class finally includes the others; all values are questions of both truth and right, while both of these are questions of good taste. All are questions of *ought* rather than *is*, in the ordinary factual meaning, though all as subjects of discussion have to be treated as objective, in contrast with subjective desire or wish. The question in every case is one of what men ought on some ground to agree about.

But for different reasons, differing judgments in the fields of beauty as commonly understood, and of truth as matter of fact rarely give rise to serious problems for social action. In esthetics, the principle of each to his own taste is usually applicable, though philosophically speaking the adage, *de gustibus non disputandum* is clearly false. And there are exceptions to the practical rule stated—in cases of public monuments and other public works where beauty takes precedence over utility. Matters of fact are in general the province of science, and where knowledge of nature is at issue, the natural sciences have tests of observation and experiment yielding conclusions acceptable to the public at large—as far and as fast as agreement is necessary. In any case, modern democracies do not undertake to determine scientific issues by making and enforcing laws. There are partial exceptions, in education; and sometimes action must be taken which involves issues controversial among scientists themselves—notably in provision for national defense. Social science is a very different matter, as I have pointed out, and I cannot here add to what I have said on that point; the essential thing is the limitations of knowledge. Whether esthetics and morals or ethics are or can be sciences is in every connection a matter of the definition of the word; judgments are pronounced in both fields that are certainly more than expressions of personal or mere taste (not arguable) and certainly are not factual on at all the level of natural-science principles. They function very differently in society—not to predict conduct but as norms for guiding choice of one end rather than another; but like predictive data, they must be known in order to implement intelligent action, and in order for social action to be agreed upon. That is the problem, particularly the knowledge problem, of greatest inherent difficulty.

The enforcement of law is in general the conservative function and, in a very general sense, is the province of criminal jurisprudence, dealing with preventive measures. While, as usual with such dichotomies there is no clear line of demarcation, the great bulk of positive action, especially of innovation, falls in the field of economic relations. As regards predictive knowledge, the consequences of measures in the latter field can be foreseen much more accurately than the effects of penalties. Economics can be much more "scientific" in the requisite sense than criminology. This is true for two reasons, as economics is really two disciplines; one deals with theory, resting on axioms and deduction, the other is empirical. Both yield fairly solid and usable knowledge, though not to be compared for accuracy or reliability with the physical sciences. (Nor even with the biological, though these are by no means on a par with physics and chemistry.) The axioms of theoretical economics are quite simple principles of instrumentally rational behavior, such as motivation by progressively satiable wants, the mutual advantage of free exchange, one price in a market, and diminishing returns from a particular resource used in combination with given amounts of others. And in the field of conduct that economists deal with, men in general tend to act rationally—and, or including, acting morally, in the sense of respecting the freedom of others. (A minimum of law is necessary, merely to prevent violence and fraud.) The main ground of empirical reliability of inferences from theory is that it is little concerned with concrete behavior—with what wants people have, or what resources they have for satisfying them, or what technology is available—but chiefly with the general structure of the organization of production and distribution that results under freedom with such given conditions. Of course the final concern in practical terms, is for its merits and defects as indicating possible improvements through politico-legal action. For application, the abstract qualitative laws must be given content from empirical study somewhat as in the case of engineering technology and theoretical physics. In this type of inquiry, results are qualified by much inaccuracy; but behavior in relation to marketable goods and services and their prices is "fairly" stable, in the mass, and it is mass behavior that is chiefly relevant for social policy. This in contrast with the effects of punishment, where society deals with individuals, and where in fact comparatively little is known even on a statistical scale.

The greater reliability of prediction of the effects of economic measures is due in part to psychology, in part to a different mode of action and different technique for enforcement. A government in power can forcibly take property or earnings away from individuals and use the proceeds to subsidize supposedly neglected activities, or to hire its own agents to perform them—or for outright gift to meet individual needs. The problem here, to repeat, is to determine (by agreement) what action is desirable, or how much, of any type recognized as needful. In criminology, the objective is not in dispute, it is to reduce crime—but preferably without recourse to the simple but harsh measure of extirpating the culprit, or the very expensive one of incarceration—and as far as feasable to reform the convicted into good citizens. The difficulties in both fields have been much intensified by the development of more humane ideals, and in criminology by psychiatric theories calling in question the concept of guilt. In economics, the justice of the productive-contribution norm of distribution is more and more doubted, in view of the gross and seemingly unmerited inequality that it creates or perpetuates, as it works out under free competition—which tends to achieve that result— in so far as the system operates in accord with its theoretical principles. Its working is, of course, greatly qualified by luck,—accidents or forces beyond human prediction or control—and diverse machinations such as monopolizing, reflecting antisocial motives, often anti-economic as well. The first task of law-and-government is to prevent the latter as far as possible, without introducing worse interferences in the long-run view, such as crippling the incentive to work, to save, and to manage effectively.

As to distributive justice, apart from the conflict of moral norms mentioned in earlier lectures—especially the impossibility of departing very far from the productivity principle —for the active participants, it must be kept in mind that these are a minor fraction of the population. It has no application to infants or dependents, who are the majority— nor does any form of freedom, correctly defined, have meaning for the helpless; for them either society or some active member of society must be responsible, economically and politically. The family is the minimum effective social unit, and a vital part of the social problem is allocating responsibility for all those who cannot—or even will not—take adequate responsibility for themselves. To keep inequality down to the minimum required for effective freedom, much must be done to offset the natural tendency to its growth, both in consumption and in power, because those who at any time have more are in a better position to acquire still more (to him that hath shall be given). Particularly offensive to individualistic ideals is the unequal start in life that results from inheritance. But it is by no means only inheritance of property that is in question—as pointed out in earlier lectures. The most important action open to society is free education of the young at the expense of the families found most able to bear the burden; and of course a great deal has been done in this respect. Again, meeting the cost is the smaller part of the problem; somebody must control the content of education and its methods—either the parents of the particular children affected or some organ of society. Many problems arise that cannot be considered here; not the least is the insistence of many parents on having their children indoctrinated with religious or ideological beliefs or prejudices that in the opinion of many others will unfit them as adults for participation in liberal institutions, political or economic.

If to act intelligently or else not act is the basic axiom for a discussion of action, the first commandment is to *compare the alternatives*. Social action means political action, which in a democracy means action by government, in accord with laws, made as well as enforced by a government consisting of persons held responsible to the people, the electorate of normal adults. The alternative is literally free action by the individual members of society or—actually, for the most part—by groups formed through voluntary association to promote common interests. But the primary unit, the family, can be only in part a voluntary group; it must be chartered by public authority and have its responsibilities largely so defined, and the same is true of most of the more important groups, up to the sovereign state, membership in which again is to a limited extent a matter of free choice. In economic relations, a close approximation to ideal voluntary association is afforded to the participants by the open market. In so far as individualistic competition is effective, no one in a market has any arbitrary power over anyone else, since each buyer or seller confronts equally good opportunities, prices being kept uniform for all by each selecting the seller or buyer who offers any detectably better terms than others. It is taken for granted that conscience or intelligence will cause each to respect the freedom of others—or that any failure to do so will be met by political action to prevent robbery or fraud. In so far as an economy, practically meaning a nation, is organized through such markets, all resources will be used so as to yield the maximum product as measured by the freely expressed preferences of consumers; and each participant in production will share in distribution to the extent of his product, the addition to the total product made by the productive resources he supplies. As already sufficiently pointed out, this system has two sets of weaknesses causing it to fall short of the ideal arrangement. First, the system for various reasons works far from perfectly as defined by the theory. Secondly, and more important, the result of such perfect competition does not conform to individualistic justice. The reasons have been indicated; the first of them is that a society is by no means made up of responsibly acting individuals, each with given wants and productive capacity. The part of the population that has these endowments at all, in varying degree, gets both predominantly from the working of social processes—indefinitely modified by luck and behavior not in accord with competitive theory—as already observed. The result of equating pay to performance depends on how both are measured, and at best the principle is justified more by necessity or expediency than by ethical idealism, which would call rather for the basis of need, or equality modified by need. Within a given enterprise the alternatives open are practically unlimited; the participants can have any arrangement on which they can agree for assigning roles and dividing up the joint product. On the method of organization, there must be agreement, free or unfree. The market system has the supreme merit of minimizing the scope of agreement; it is the only method that allows individuals free choice as consumers and producers, with the need to agree only on the method itself.

In contrast, governmental action cannot be comparably free. At the limit, a majority must dictate to minorities— and in political reality nothing like majority decision— opinion or will, or both—can be made effective on specific issues. And still less on what issues are to come to a vote and in what form. Further, there are severe limitations on the process of discussion, which is the democratic method of reaching agreement. Lord Bryce defined democracy as "government by discussion," and genuine discussion is the ideal type of free association, its defining exemplification. To begin with, it depends on *inter*communication, which on any considerable scale is impossible, and any close approach is almost infinitely slow and tedious. For, while one person can communicate to a large number, even by word-of-mouth —and to any number by using modern technical aids (if they will listen)—one cannot listen to or read communication from but one other at a time; and no scientific discovery or invention can change that fact. Some approximation to ideal discussion is possible in very small groups—assuming a common language, and a general agreement on courtesy and the will to observe its requirements, and allowing time. And the general result may be somewhat approached on a larger scale through overlapping of small groups and mobility of their membership—and again if enough time is available. Besides these limitations, formal discussion on a considerable scale (and subject to time limits) must be *organized*, and this presupposes both law—rules of order— and an authority with power for enforcing the rules. Thus there is a circular or hen-and-egg relation between law-and-leadership, the essentials of social order, and the activity by which either or both can be "freely" improved or changed. It will be evident that even in the "mechanics" there are quite narrow limits to the amount, and especially the speed, of change that be intelligently effected.

One of the hardest questions in defining freedom is that of the extent to which it requires "intelligence" in the first place, specifically knowledge of the possible alternative modes of action and their consequences for the more or less distant future. All purposive action looks to the future, and intelligent social action must consider the interests and well-being of future members—not only the living infants but generations unborn, and all the values embodied in a high civilization, and the progressively higher level to be achieved. In so far as knowledge of alternatives of choice and their consequences is requisite for social freedom, another sweeping "limitation" is set by the fact that a group must act through individual agents, specifically that laws are both administered and made by human persons. Ideally, these agents act under law and are responsible to the people as a whole, that is, to public opinion and will—the will to act intelligently, in accord with knowledge of values. But agents must have more or less discretion in action; it is self-contradictory that laws should accurately cover every detail, and wholly unrealistic to imagine that laws approximately prescribing details could be obeyed, or would be. Our political tradition has been marked by a grossly one-sided emphasis on government by laws and not by men, as well as on laws being made by "the people." If there is unanimity on what the laws ought to be, formal law will be superfluous—or we are relegated to the medieval conception that sin is the only ground of need for stating and enforcing the laws.

Not only in government is the agency relation fundamental; it is ubiquitous in the conduct of any organization,
and even in personal relations on the smallest scale and
without formal organization. Prior to the fact of organization, it is an inevitable result of the specialization of knowledge, which in turn is a necessary condition of the growth of
knowledge and activity for its advancement. Again the field
of medicine may be drawn upon for an illustration at the
simplest level, the relation between a patient and his doctor.
The freedom possible to the patient is that of choosing his
doctor in the first place, and changing doctors at will. The
relation once established, the agent has *power* over the
patient—in this case power of life-and-death. That is extreme,
but the principles are the same for all expert and consultant
relations and these, to repeat, are inevitable at every turn in
a free-and-progressive society. Not only does the agent in
such relations inevitably have power, over his principal—he
cannot be very intelligently selected by the latter. The
patient would have to know extant medical science—largely
obviating his need for the service (which begins with telling
him whether he needs it or not) and in addition know both
the technical qualifications and the moral reliability of the
available candidates for the role. The selection, and the
terms on which the services of an agent are provided, must
in a free society be determined by competition—specifically
market competition—and this is necessarily very imperfect.
(Even when not made more so by collusive "monopolistic"
action, which is strikingly familiar in medical practice.)

The problem is indefinitely more complex and difficult
when an organization must be "represented" by an agent
the group must select. As things work out, the active
competition is chiefly on the side of would-be agents seeking

principals, who usually play a more passive role. In the case of government, the major task of organization is to provide means for forming and expressing the public opinion for which its personnel are to speak and act. A free society cannot at all get rid of either tradition or authority; the freedom of the individual—besides being limited by his character, a set of habits built up in the milieu of a tradition— is mainly that of choosing the authority he will respect and follow, that is, his boss. This applies to the intellectual life as well as to conduct. Most of what anyone believes is derived either from tradition or from some authority. It is of the essence of freedom to place the individual in the paradoxical position of judging between persons who admittedly are more competent on the issues than he is himself. And every organization, including the state as the whole people, is in the same position, in one way and degree or another. All face the necessity of somehow agreeing on the selection of persons for positions of authority, and on the powers to be formally conferred.

The most important case, and most misunderstood, is that of organized productive enterprise or the business unit in whatever form it takes. Modern technology requires that both production and exchange be conducted by units of varying but in general substantial size and complexity, and requires that these be managed by persons who must have a large amount of discretionary power. In the free economy, ultimate control is vested in an entrepreneur who himself largely acts through agents responsible to him (or it, a comparatively small group); but the main fact is that at the same time the entrepreneur acts as the agent of the consumers of the product and of the workers and property-owners who furnish the productive services used in the operations. Here as in the case of the medical patient, the choice consonant with freedom is the selection, subject to market competition, among those who must make the concrete decisions involved in production and the sharing of the result. To be free, all must act individually; any collusion will both reduce efficiency and lead to conflicts of interest which can be settled only by force. To some extent, indeed, government may act to secure more effective responsibility—as it undertakes to do in the case of medical practice. In general, the main useful action will be to preserve the conditions of effective market competition—or, where this is not feasible, to replace the mechanism of the market by some politically chosen authority.

Other things must be done, along more positive lines. Much compulsory redistribution of income is necessary, in comparison with the "natural" working of the market order, in addition to suppressing monopoly or monopoloid arrangements—where they are on balance a serious evil, and where it can be done with a net balance of good over harm in the result. Both problems are extremely difficult, as was pointed out in earlier lectures. With respect to redistribution, less inequality of income is undoubtedly to be prescribed, but at least as important is prevention of excessive concentration of power. And that is a far more complex and difficult problem, especially since political action calls for centralization of power in the state. The only procedure compatible with the principles of a free society is equitable taxation and judicious use of the proceeds. Arbitrary price-fixing for any good or service is rarely if ever defensible, and only (if ever) as a method of dealing with natural monopolies less inexpedient than public ownership. It is almost always bad when done legally by the government, in the best possible way, and is categorically indefensible if the government passively or actively delegates the power to any special interest group with a direct financial stake in the result. The primary function of law and government is preventive action to prohibit exploitation or any form of coercion by any individual, group, or class against any other. It must monopolize coercion and itself use coercion primarily in this negative sense.

Chiefly in point is the utmost obstruction of organizations aimed at power rather than harmonious efficiency. On the current scene the main special interests in question are business, labor, and the farmer. The evils and dangers of business power are small in comparison with the other two interests, for the *prima-facie* reason that they have long been recognized and discussed and much legislation and administrative action directed to counteracting them. This evil has been generally much exaggerated, in comparison with the others, with the result that much action—as well as much failure to act—has been palpably unwise. In economic terms, the evil is monopoly, and it is immaterial whether restriction is directly applied to a price or to the quantity of supply of a good or service offered in the market. The deeper root of discriminative action against "business" is an inveterate traditional prejudice against that form of power, in favor of practically any other form, disregarding our first commandment to compare alternatives intelligently. The public seem to assume that monopolizing is virtuous when practiced by anybody else against business, and wicked on the part of the latter alone. Vastly more costly to society are the monopolies conducted by the other two interests, with the approval of public opinion and the connivance or direct support of the government. Fortunately, in a sense, the farm program in this country is the more palpably absurd and has been carried to such lengths as apparently to produce some reaction in public opinion that may lead to some approach to horse-sense in that field. The imbecilities of the past generation would of course be impossible without the approval of many who pay for them as well as those immediately benefited—who in general are persons with no claim to charity and who get it largely at the expense of others worse off— the general consumer.

The supreme menace to the social-economic well-being and obstacle to good sense in public economic policy is the increasing arbitrary power of organized labor, and the gross unwisdom with which it is used, in terms of the economic interest of wage-earners themselves, apart from the exploitative ethics of what is attempted and in considerable part achieved. The spokesmen for labor consistently demand more and more for less and less, in terms of effort or skill, and seem to care hardly at all about who pays, even immediately, and still less in the longer run. Statistics show wages to be somewhat higher in strongly unionized employments; but this is no indication that it is not because they are reduced in other employments, and takes no account of the negative effect on total output and the loss inflicted on consumers. Even if it could be shown that workers as a class gain something for the time being, at the expense of property-owners— as it cannot be and as is probably not true—the effect on economic progress is the far more serious consideration, and hardly comes into the discussion at all. The most depressing feature of the situation is the character of the arguments used to support the claim for more now, and the fact that they go with the public, even with the spokesmen for the employer interest. Rather the worst is the use of the productivity concept, crediting the operative personnel with all the fruits of increased investment per operative, of technological progress, and even of the rapidly increasing input of managerial white-collar effort. But no better analytically is the pretense of a right to an arbitrarily defined scale of living at the expense of the particular employer. It is essentially self-evident that the only valid claim to wages is the value of the product to the able and willing buyer for consumption; and another truth at the same level is that labor cannot get more in a free economy over a considerable period of time, and will get less as the result of any coercive effort to get more. For, in a society with elementary economic freedom, men cannot be forced into the role of employing labor on any terms that fall short of an inducement satisfactory to themselves. And no more can free men be forced to accumulate wealth and put it to productive use.

On the other hand, of course, overt coercion will not make men work effectively at the more routine occupations. Abolition of slavery finally depended on that fact. The indispensable condition for a free and progressive economy is a general understanding of the possibilities, and a reasonable degree of contentment with what can be done and be had—especially in a long-run view. Nor does what I have said about the grasping and overreaching attitude of farmers and wage-earners—instead of using their freedom to transfer to other roles—at all imply that the property or management interests are exempt from the same criticism. But as things stand, in the existing state of public opinion, what the latter can get away with is little in comparison with the other two. Nor, finally, is it implied that government should take no action looking to more equitable distribution of the fruits of social progress. But this is as true of the costs of progress, a seriously neglected subject. What is most depressing, I repeat, is the nonsensical arguments used on all sides, to further a struggle for power to get more, at the expense of no-matter-whom. But, again, it is stupid for believers in democracy to blame anybody for using the arguments that work with the general public, short of outright fraud, and still less for taking the action of which the public approves. Probably the supreme economic stupidity—real prejudice— generally held is the idea that employees are working for the bosses, any more than these are working for the employees. All are working for themselves, indirectly and far more effectively by working for one another—which is the nature and supreme merit of exchange relations. Yet patients tend to take the same attitude toward the doctor, and students not uncommonly talk as if they were working for the teacher—and act more or less as if they believe it— and feel no obligation to charity in the matter. The only remedy for such nonsense is more general intelligence, beginning with the will to attack problems intelligently. Both must be produced—if there is any effective treatment—by education, in a broad meaning. But in a democracy the public must and will educate itself, the future public, in the direction it chooses, which makes the final issue that of the will to be intelligent.

This lecture and the series may close on the rather sad note that the supreme basic obstacle to progress is the human disposition to see conditions in moral terms, and moralize about them. People habitually look for someone to *blame* for any supposed wrong or ill, and to *punish* as the remedy. Liberal culture inherited from the Middle Ages the "sin theory" of evil in general; and in the form this has taken, it can do more damage than formerly when it led to seeking personal salvation rather than mundane social change. The worst manifestation is the two-fold blaming business for economic conditions judged unideal, and as naively holding the government responsible for fixing whatever a snap judgment finds wrong. The least objective consideration must show that democratic politics works in much the same general way as business—it is much more ruled by the motive of competitive persuasion, the contest spirit—and can do far more damage. If free society is to persist, or improve, the people must learn that problems are to be solved only by intelligent agreement through genuine free discussion—beginning with identification of those that are real and soluble and struggling with these rather than quarreling over evils that are unreal or palpably in the nature of things and hence irremediable. Being good, in conventional, romantic, and dogmatic terms, is no solution, and forcing others to be good has a very limited place and is dangerously liable to be disastrously overdone. A people that thinks the way to benefit workers is to treat employers as their enemy, persecute them, and make the role as unattractive as possible does not deserve freedom and cannot expect to have it indefinitely. The possibilities of freedom in effectively organized society have sweeping limitations; but accepting these and working intelligently within their bounds, and not too discontentedly, is the price of the residual freedom that is possible, and that is still the most precious boon of life.

INDEX